IMAGES
of America

THE PHOENIX AREA'S PARKS AND PRESERVES

PAPAGO PARK, PHOENIX, ARIZONA

An iconic landmark for the Phoenix area is the red rock buttes within Papago Park. The unusual rock formations and spectacular desert vegetation made this park one of the most popular in the metropolitan area, also known as the "Valley of the Sun," and the first area targeted for preservation. (Courtesy Arizona Historical Foundation, Phoenix Area Subject Photograph Collection, No. DPX-131.)

ON THE COVER: The spectacular mountain scenery that surrounds the Phoenix area has exerted a powerful draw on both Phoenicians and tourists. In this photograph from the early 1920s, a truly special picnic is enjoyed near the base of Squaw Peak. (Courtesy Arizona Historical Foundation, Gusse Thomas Smith Photograph Collection, No. GTS-35.)

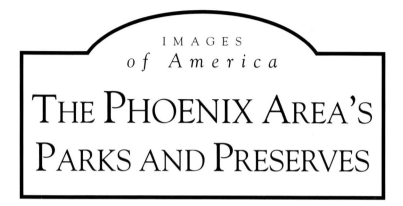

IMAGES
of America

THE PHOENIX AREA'S PARKS AND PRESERVES

Donna and George Hartz

Arizona Historical Foundation

ARCADIA
PUBLISHING

Copyright © 2007 by Donna and George Hartz
ISBN 978-0-7385-4886-9

Published by Arcadia Publishing
Charleston, South Carolina

Printed in the United States of America

Library of Congress Catalog Card Number: 2006939744

For all general information contact Arcadia Publishing at:
Telephone 843-853-2070
Fax 843-853-0044
E-mail sales@arcadiapublishing.com
For customer service and orders:
Toll-Free 1-888-313-2665

Visit us on the Internet at www.arcadiapublishing.com

To our children and grandchildren—with whom we share memories of many outings to the Phoenix area's parks and preserves.

CONTENTS

ACKNOWLEDGMENTS

We entered into this project as complete novices in the field of historical photographs, hoping that interesting images could be found to help us tell the story of the creation of the magnificent system of parks and preserves within the Phoenix area. To the extent we were successful, it is due to the kindness and support given to us by so many people at some 20 different organizations.

The professional archivists and librarians patiently educated us on the collection and preservation of historical photographs. Much thanks to Jack August, Jared Jackson, and the team at the Arizona Historical Foundation; to Rob Spindler and his team at the Arizona Room of the Arizona State University (ASU) Hayden Library; to Leigh Conrad and Steven Defrates from the Southwest Room of the Scottsdale Public Library; to Beth Brand at the Desert Botanical Garden; to JoAnn Handley at the Scottsdale Historical Society; to David Tatum and Dawn Nave at the Arizona Historical Society Museum at Papago Park in Tempe; to Joe Abodeely at Papago Park's Arizona Military Museum; and to Michael Smith from the CCC Alumni organization.

We received tremendous assistance from a number of individuals in locating historical photographs from within the parks' own collections. At the top of that list is David Urbinato, the public information officer at the Phoenix Parks and Recreation Department, who managed to locate several boxes of old photographs, slides, and negatives from their storage facilities and allowed us to set up shop in their conference room over several days while we explored, sorted, and scanned. Rhonda Woodward of the Maricopa County Parks and Recreation Department similarly located and shared a couple of boxes of old photographs. Don Meserve with Scottsdale's Preservation Division shared many hundreds of photographs with us, and Bob Cafarella located a photograph of a particularly important event. Carla from the McDowell Sonoran Conservancy generously shared that organization's photograph archives, and Aimee Yamamori at the Phoenix Zoo assembled a collection of slides for us. Gary Driggs shared his memories and expertise on both Camelback Mountain and the Phoenix Mountain Preserve.

Finally, our thanks to the thousands of residents of the Phoenix area who dreamed great dreams, raised their voices, and fought the fights necessary to give us the spectacular collection of parks and preserves we so much need and enjoy today.

INTRODUCTION

New York has its skyline, San Francisco its bridge and bay, Seattle has its Space Needle . . .
Phoenix has jagged mountain peaks, majestic saguaro cacti and sweeping desert vistas. Within
the urbanized area itself and visible to most urban residents on a daily basis, are prominent desert
landmarks such as Camelback Mountain, South Mountain Park, Piestewa Peak (formerly known as
Squaw Peak), the Dreamy Draw and Papago Park's popular Hole in the Rock. It is significant that
Phoenix uses natural rather than human landmarks as a way of presenting itself to the outside world
in defining a collective identity."

—Patricia Gober
Metropolitan Phoenix: Place Making and Community Building in the Desert, 2005, pages 5–6
(Reprinted with permission of the University of Pennsylvania Press)

At the beginning of 1914, Phoenix was a modest-sized city of about 23,000 people, occupying a bit over 3,300 acres of land. Maricopa County's population was only slightly more than 50,000. Phoenix was surrounded by large tracts of agricultural land and seemingly endless miles of beautiful, unspoiled Sonoran desert and spectacular mountain scenery. Open space was everywhere.

Given these conditions, one would not expect that spending political capital or taxpayer's money on open space preservation would have been a high priority for Phoenix's citizens, political leaders, or community activists. Yet, over the next 10 years, Phoenix's leaders would aggressively lobby the federal government to create a park of 2,000-plus acres around the Papago Buttes five miles east of downtown, plus buy more than 14,500 acres to create what is often described as the country's largest municipal park in what were then known as the Salt River Mountains.

The creation of these parks is a story of great vision and foresight on the part of Phoenix's citizens and leaders, and it provides an excellent example of the importance of municipal open space preservation—even when it appears that there is plenty of open space at hand.

Today few would argue the value of preserving open space in and around our rapidly growing urban centers. For many of Arizona's urban residents, their sense of place is still strongly tied to the deserts and the mountains. As the deserts are plowed under and the mountains become dotted with homes, an important part of one's Arizona identity becomes more remote. After all, open space is essential to Arizonans' sense of place.

Unfortunately, today the competition for the remaining open space is intense and conflicted by residential development, commercial expansion, parks/preserves, etc. The City of Scottsdale may spend more than $500 million in acquiring 36,400 acres of land for its McDowell Sonoran Preserve while foregoing tax revenue from homes and businesses that could have occupied that land.

This book celebrates this foresight and determination of the citizens and leaders in the Phoenix area who, throughout the 20th century, conceived, acquired, and built the terrific collection of parks and preserves that hold so much meaning, not only the nearly four million people who now live in Maricopa County, but also to countless visitors to the area each year. The region encompassing metropolitan Phoenix has now protected, or has plans to protect, over 200,000 acres (more than 300 square miles), much of it through the efforts of local residents and local taxes, including residents who voted to raise their taxes for the purpose of protecting "their" land.

The book focuses on several of the largest and most noteworthy of the Phoenix area's parks and preserves. Chapter one looks at the creation of Papago Saguaro National Monument in 1914 and its evolution into the Papago Park of today. Chapter two focuses on the 1924 acquisition of over 14,000 acres in the Salt River Mountains from the federal government and the creation of what is now called South Mountain Park/Preserve. Chapter three describes the creation of Encanto Park during the 1930s and the achievement of the long-sought major pleasure park for Phoenix. Chapter four illustrates the establishment of Estrella Mountain Regional Park in 1954 and the ensuing establishment of a ring of large and impressive mountain parks by Maricopa County. Chapter five presents the decade-long effort of concerned citizens and civic leaders to protect that symbol of Phoenix—Camelback Mountain. Chapter six chronicles the effort of Phoenix citizens in the 1950s and 1960s to protect large areas of the Phoenix Mountains, particularly what was then known as Squaw Peak. Chapter seven concludes the book with a review of the grassroots efforts from the 1990s through the present day to preserve nearly one-third of Scottsdale's total land area as the McDowell Sonoran Preserve.

We are happy to celebrate this amazing collection of Phoenix area parks and preserves and to showcase the imagination, determination, and deep love for the majestic vistas and open spaces that have so clearly defined our sense of place as Arizonans during the past century.

One

PAPAGO PARK

Papago Park has the longest and most complex history of the major parks or preserves within the Phoenix area. Early residents and community leaders knew that they wanted the land containing the Papago Buttes saved for the public. How it was to be saved and how it was to be used were questions whose answers long remained unclear. At the beginning of the 20th century, the quickest and cheapest way to save the land was withdrawal by the federal government, but that posed challenges that were not fully appreciated. In many ways, the ongoing story of Papago Park is the story of a community struggling to balance civic, recreational, and preservation desires within the real world context of economic practicalities. There was never a lack of ideas, nor a lack of desire to make it work. It remains an incredible asset to the Phoenix area and is a story with chapters still to be written.

PAPAGO PARK

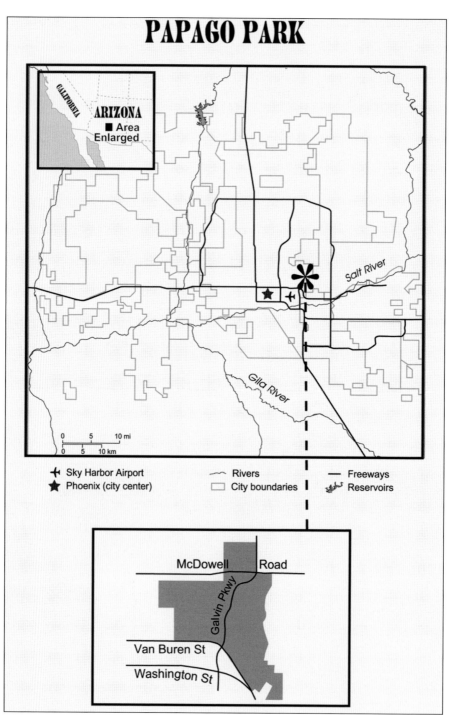

Papago Park is located in the southeastern part of Phoenix and the northern part of Tempe. It also shares a long border with Scottsdale, giving all three cities a great interest in its prosperity. The main road through Papago Park is Galvin Parkway, which can be reached from E. McDowell Road to the north and from E. Van Buren Street to the south. Twenty percent of the park (about 300 acres) is in Tempe, and the remaining 1,200 acres are in Phoenix. (Map by Donna Hartz.)

The landscape of what is now known as Papago Park is dominated by a series of large, red rock buttes. These sedimentary sandstone formations were formed between 6 and 15 million years ago and sit directly upon the bedrock, which is exposed at places throughout the park. (Courtesy Scottsdale Public Library's Southwest Collection.)

In 1879, Pres. Rutherford B. Hayes included the Papago Buttes area in a new reservation for the Salt River Pima Maricopa Indians. After much local opposition, President Hayes in 1880 moved the western boundary of the reservation two miles to the east, and the Papago Buttes area remained within the public domain. Several claims were filed by settlers for the Papago Buttes area in the late 1880s and early 1890s, but these were eventually rejected and cancelled. (Courtesy Arizona Historical Foundation, Phoenix Area Subject Photograph Collection, No. DPX-167.)

Perhaps the best known of the rock formations in what is now known as Papago Park is Hole-in-the-Rock. Eons of erosion and weathering have resulted in a large opening in the butte, easily accessible from the eastern side. (Courtesy Scottsdale Public Library's Southwest Collection.)

The views from Hole-in-the-Rock are spectacular. This early-20th-century view to the west includes the city of Phoenix, as well as the beautiful backdrop of the Salt River Mountains (South Mountain), the Estrella Mountains, and the White Tank Mountains. (Courtesy Scottsdale Public Library's Southwest Collection.)

The Hole-in-the-Rock area was a magnet for the early residents of Phoenix and the surrounding communities for outings, picnics, and photographs. One of the ladies in this 1897 picture is identified as Bessie Copes. She and her friend, dressed in their finest, posed for this special photograph. (Courtesy Herb and Dorothy McLaughlin Collection, Arizona State University Libraries.)

Family and friends looked forward to the special occasion of the Hole-in-the-Rock excursion, and whenever possible, recorded the moment for posterity. This picture from the early 20th century is typical of the photographs from this era. (Courtesy Scottsdale Public Library's Southwest Collection.)

The Papago area has much more than just the popular Hole-in-the-Rock, and this early photograph records the excitement of reaching the top of one of the buttes. It is interesting to observe the variety of climbing outfits chosen for the excursion. (Courtesy Scottsdale Public Library's Southwest Collection.)

Hole-in-the-Rock has remained a popular spot for romance, despite the presence of graffiti along its walls. The amazing views and easy accessibility make it the perfect place for a romantic picnic, especially with a photograph to remember the occasion. However, by the end of the first decade of the 20th century, the rapidly growing Phoenix area exposed the Papago Buttes area to development. (Courtesy Scottsdale Public Library's Southwest Collection.)

In 1902, certain land within the Papago Buttes area was withdrawn from the public domain for use by the Salt River Valley Water Users Association (referred to in this text by its modern name of Salt River Project [SRP]) in furtherance of their irrigation- and power-generation activities. In 1913, SRP opened their crosscut canal between the Arizona Canal and the Salt River, along the eastern side of the Papago area. They also announced plans for the construction of two hydroelectric plants in Papago (pictured above). The construction of the canal spurred increased homesteading interest in the immediate area. (Courtesy Library of Congress.)

In 1909, another parcel of land in the Papago Buttes area was withdrawn from the public domain for the creation of a rifle range for the Arizona National Guard. This picture from 1915 shows troops practicing at the Papago Rifle Range. By the beginning of the 1910s, more and more citizens and community leaders began to fear the loss of the Papago Buttes to continuing development pressure. (Courtesy Arizona Historical Society, No. 74.33.117 [No. 1064].)

The pressure to create public recreation areas led Arizona congressional delegate Ralph Cameron to introduce legislation in 1911 to set aside a huge tract of nearly 13,000 acres; but Arizona was not yet a state, and nothing happened. After statehood in 1912, Carl Hayden became Arizona's lone member of the U.S. House of Representatives, and he led the fight to preserve the Papago Buttes area. Hayden, pictured at left, was from Tempe, immediately across the river from the area and was well aware of the area's importance to the local citizens. First he introduced legislation to create a park of about 1,500 acres but got nowhere. He then pushed for the creation of a Cactus National Park at Papago but was rebuffed by the Department of Interior. (Courtesy Arizona Historical Foundation, Carl Hayden Photograph Collection, No. CH-81.)

In 1913, Hayden, a Democrat, was finding friends in the new administration of Democratic president Woodrow Wilson (pictured at right). The Department of Interior agreed to explore the creation of a new national monument at Papago. The Antiquities Act of 1906 gave the president the authority to proclaim National Monuments from federally owned land that contained items of unique scientific interest. Twelve such monuments had already been proclaimed, including six in Arizona. On January 31, 1914, President Wilson issued a proclamation creating Papago Saguaro National Monument (PSNM)—2,053.43 acres. This included the buttes and large stands of saguaro cacti. The area was now safe from development, or so it seemed. (Courtesy Library of Congress.)

The Phoenix area now had its first major park, but initially nothing much changed. Congress provided minimal funding for improvements, while the public clamored for recreational amenities such as a golf course, swimming pool, tennis courts, etc. The park remained popular with 5,000 visitors in 1920 and 8,000 in 1922. In addition to visits to Hole-in-the-Rock, such as D.C. Smith's pictured above from the early 1920s, PSNM was also used for other activities, such as church services and weddings. The National Park Service (NPS) was becoming unhappy about the local pressure for improvements and nontraditional usages. (Courtesy Herb and Dorothy McLaughlin Collection, Arizona State University Libraries.)

PSNM remains an idyllic place to visit and a great backdrop against which to be photographed, such as it was for this young girl in the early 1920s. However, local citizens constantly pressured the NPS for more local control and more varied usage. In 1923, Pres. Warren G. Harding began reducing the park bit by bit for such things as a railroad crossing, road building, and even shale mining, eventually reducing PSNM to 1,940 acres. It became increasingly clear that locals and national leaders had diverging views on what it meant to be a national monument. (Courtesy Scottsdale Historical Society.)

Differing viewpoints for the national monument reached crisis level in the late 1920s, when the Arizona Game and Fish Department began pushing for the building of a bass fish hatchery within PSNM. Although this was seriously debated within the NPS, most in Washington felt this use was completely inappropriate. Talk began over the possibility of abolishing the national monument. Seen above, the bass fish hatchery was built in the early 1930s, and by 1936, it produced 175,000 bass and another 175,000 perch annually. (Courtesy Tempe Historical Society.)

Talk of abandoning the monument became more serious, and in 1926 the secretary of interior suggested to then-governor George Hunt that the monument should be decommissioned and turned over to either the state or city. Senator Hayden introduced legislation in 1928 and again in 1929, and it successfully passed Congress April 7, 1930. Pres. Herbert Hoover, seen at left, signed the law. PSNM land was distributed among several entities. Most of the land went to the state, with a much smaller amount transferred to the City of Tempe (both for no cost), and the land already being used by SRP was sold to SRP for a relatively modest $1.25 per acre. The Phoenix area got what it wanted—Papago Park—with most of the Papago Buttes area preserved for public recreation at no cost to the taxpayers and without the troublesome interference from the federal government. (Courtesy Library of Congress.)

The early 1930s saw the continuation of some nontraditional uses for the park. George Hunt, who served seven terms as Arizona's governor, was buried on a hilltop within the park. A pyramid-shaped tomb marks its location, not far from Hole-in-the-Rock. (Courtesy Hartz family.)

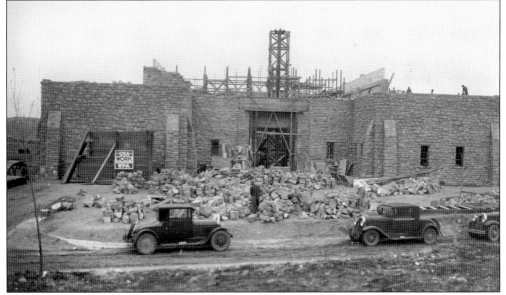

The northwest portion of the park remained important to the military. It was in this area that the National Guard rifle range was built in 1909, and in the mid-1930s, the federal Works Progress Administration (WPA) assisted in the construction of a large adobe arsenal for the National Guard. Pictured above during construction, the arsenal now houses the Arizona Military Museum. (Courtesy Arizona Military Museum.)

During the 1930s, the federal Civilian Conservation Corps (CCC) established a camp in Papago Park. The CCC built a boathouse and dock at the fish hatchery, an amphitheater, grills, fireplaces, ramadas, roads, and trails. This 1938 photograph shows Ruth Wilson and friends enjoying a day in Papago Park and taking advantage of CCC-built amenities. (Courtesy Fred Wilson Collection, Arizona Collection, Arizona State University Libraries.)

Despite all the traditional and nontraditional activities within Papago Park, it remained a place of great natural beauty, even though some scenes, such as this one of the lake in a 1930s photograph, is not natural desert scenery. (Courtesy Madge Rushton Photographs, Arizona Collection, Arizona State University Libraries.)

The disappearance of so much of the natural desert scenery within Papago Park was of growing concern to a small group of people. One such person was Gustaf Starck (seen at right), an engineer with SRP and an advocate for protecting desert flora, particularly cacti. With the redevelopment of the former Papago Saguaro National Monument, Starck and other like-minded citizens sought ways to save and preserve the remaining native desert vegetation both within and outside the park. They formed the Arizona Cactus and Native Flora Society on April 18, 1934. (Courtesy Library Archives, Desert Botanical Garden.)

Another leader of this citizenly effort was Gertrude Divine Webster (pictured at left). Webster was a wealthy resident of the valley who had an interest in cacti, which brought her into contact with Starck. She joined the Arizona Cactus and Native Flora Society and became its president in 1936. (Courtesy Library Archives, Desert Botanical Garden.)

The society quickly focused on land within Papago Park for its desired botanical garden. The land was owned by the state and administered by the Department of Game and Fish. Fortunately Gertrude Webster and her friends had considerable political savvy and influence. On July 1, 1938, the state granted the society land within the park for a botanical garden. Work began immediately, and a ground-breaking ceremony attended by more 200 people was held February 12, 1939, to officially dedicate the Desert Botanical Garden. Gertrude Webster is shown in this photograph from May 1939. (Courtesy Library Archives, Desert Botanical Garden.)

The Desert Botanical Garden benefited from hundreds of cactus specimens donated by Starck, Webster, and others. Webster, writing about the establishment of the garden, outlined a threefold purpose—to conserve Arizona desert flora, to establish scientific plantings for students and botanists, and to create a compelling attraction for winter visitors. This photograph is from the May 1939 ground breaking of what became the Webster Auditorium. (Courtesy Library Archives, Desert Botanical Garden.)

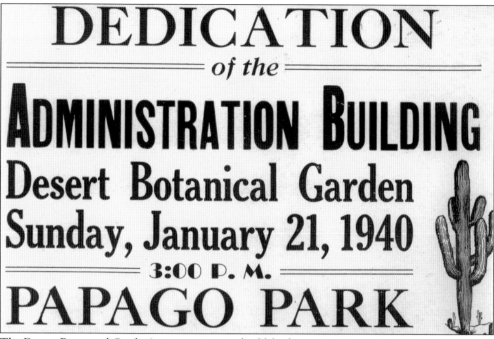

The Desert Botanical Garden's next step was to build facilities necessary to carry out their mission, specifically a library, meeting rooms, and offices. Funds were publicly raised for the large adobe building erected in 1939. Reflecting the increased public interest in the garden, nearly 2,000 people attended the dedication of the Webster Auditorium on January 21, 1940. (Courtesy Library Archives, Desert Botanical Garden.)

As can be seen from the aerial photograph from the 1940s, the basic structure of the Desert Botanical Gardens was in place with paths winding through collections of over 5,000 specimens. Unfortunately world events would soon dominate both the country and the activities at Papago Park. (Courtesy Library Archives, Desert Botanical Garden.)

Company "D", 120th QM Regiment, Papago Park, July, 1940

The story of Papago Park during the war years of the 1940s is dominated by the presence and expansion of military activities. This photograph from 1940 shows a National Guard company assembling in front of the adobe arsenal building. During World War II, the War Department requisitioned all of Papago Park except the Desert Botanical Garden, picnic grounds, and the fish hatchery. (Courtesy Arizona Military Museum.)

Additional barracks facilities were erected in Papago Park to house the growing number of troops, both before and after the establishment of the prisoner of war (POW) camp. This photograph shows a typical barracks scene. (Courtesy Arizona Historical Society, No. 90.139.9.)

Papago Park was selected for the establishment of a POW camp. In 1943, the first POWs, mostly Italian, arrived at Papago Park. By January 1944, the Papago camp had been designated solely for German POWs, primarily from the German navy. In March 1944, the prisoner population reached its maximum at 3,100. By the end of 1944, the camp received notoriety because of its POW escape. Here the entrance to the escape tunnel is seen. (Courtesy Arizona State Library, Archives and Public Records, Archives Division, Phoenix, No. 99-9159.)

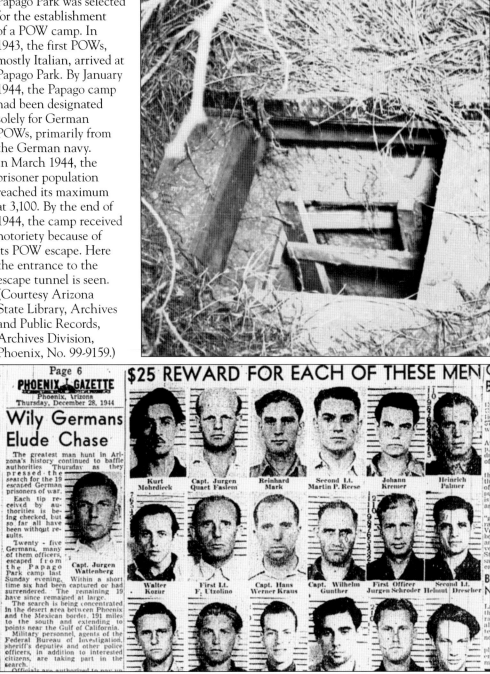

On December 23, 1944, the largest escape from a United States POW camp occurred at the Papago camp. Prisoners dug a 178-foot tunnel to the SRP crosscut canal. The POWs intended to use rafts they had built to float down the Salt River, not realizing it was frequently dry. Above is the *Phoenix Gazette*'s announcement of a reward for capture of the escaped POWs. None of the POWs got far, as all were eventually caught within the Phoenix area. (Courtesy Arizona State Library, Archives and Public Records, Archives Division, Phoenix, No. 99-9459.)

After the war ended, it took much effort over many years to return Papago Park to its status as a public recreation facility. The Desert Botanical Garden suffered extensive deterioration during the war years, and its treasury was nearly depleted. But by the early 1950s, it had worked its way back. This photograph from 1951 shows R. C. and Claire Meyer Proctor, well-known and broadly published desert photographers. They lived in the Phoenix area and were very active in the Desert Botanical Garden, the setting of this photograph, which shows a return to some normalcy. (Courtesy Library Archives, Desert Botanical Garden.)

This 1954 aerial photograph of Desert Botanical Gardens shows that it is well on its way to full recovery, though future prosperity would be dependent on improvements to the entire Papago Park area. As can be seen from this photograph, minimal visitor support infrastructure was in place around the Desert Botanical Garden. (Courtesy Library Archives, Desert Botanical Garden.)

State and local leaders realized that Papago Park desperately needed attention and direction. In December 1956, the Phoenix Planning Commission issued a report containing a comprehensive series of recommendations to turn Papago Park into a major, full-scale recreational facility for both residents and tourists. Although not all recommendations came to fruition, Papago Park was finally on the road to recovery. (Courtesy Phoenix Parks and Recreation Department.)

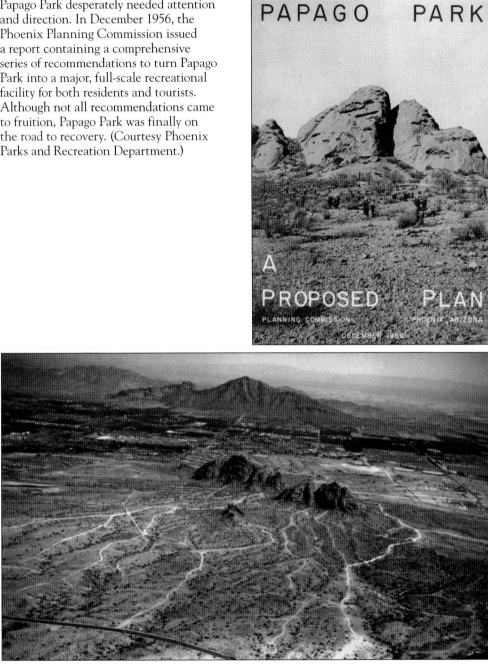

A key priority was a switch in management from the Arizona Game and Fish Department to the City of Phoenix. This was accomplished in the form of a required "public" auction on February 25, 1959, and reopened in August 1960 under the auspices of the Phoenix Parks Department. As this 1957 aerial photograph shows, access within the park was limited but was greatly improved with the construction of Galvin Parkway in 1962. (Courtesy Herb and Dorothy McLaughlin Collection, Arizona State University Libraries.)

Priorities for improvement included cleaning the park of the signs of decades of neglect and vandalism. This photograph shows a graffiti removal project from the 1960s. This period saw the closing of the fish hatchery and the conversion of that area to improved picnic grounds. Papago Park also saw improvements to the hiking and equestrian trails and the addition of various sports facilities. (Courtesy Phoenix Parks and Recreation Department.)

Ground was broken in March 1963 for construction of the Papago Golf Course, shown shortly after its opening. Phoenix Municipal Stadium opened in 1964, providing a venue for spring training and other entertainment, such as concerts. (Courtesy Phoenix Parks and Recreation Department.)

One of the 1956 plan's priorities was creating a zoo within Papago Park. Although voters approved a bond issue in 1957 for Papago Park improvements, it did not include money for a zoo. Fortunately, Robert Maytag (pictured at right), from the Maytag appliance family, was a passionate supporter of zoos and agreed to lead a private development effort. (Courtesy Phoenix Zoo.)

In 1961, Maytag and others founded the Phoenix Zoological Society, which began planning and fund-raising efforts under the slogan "Build a Zoo in '62". (Courtesy Phoenix Zoo.)

Ground was broken in Papago Park for the new "Maytag Zoo" in 1962 through an agreement with the City of Phoenix. This photograph shows some of the early construction. Sadly Maytag did not live to see his dream come true. He died unexpectedly six months prior to the zoo's opening, and his wife, Nancy, took over leadership efforts. (Courtesy Phoenix Zoo.)

Construction of the zoo involved extensive modification of the natural desert environment, and extensive relandscaping was required. This photograph from the preopening period shows the early stages of the landscaping effort. (Courtesy Phoenix Zoo.)

In November 1962, the Maytag Zoo officially opened, fulfilling the dream to "Build a Zoo in '62". Nancy Maytag performs the ribbon-cutting ceremony. From the beginning, the zoo included a children's zoo and an Arizona exhibit, and featured Hazel and Congo, two infant gorillas. (Courtesy Phoenix Zoo.)

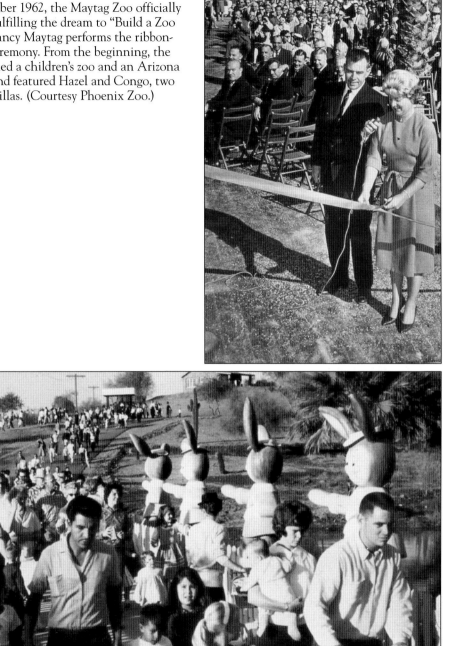

Although the opening day crowds, pictured, were enthusiastic, the zoo struggled financially. In 1963, the zoo's name was changed to the Phoenix Zoo in hopes of broadening community support. Progress was slow but steady, with the zoo increasing in size, attendance, and animal diversity. By the early 21st century, the zoo had more than 1,200 animals and about 1.2 million visitors annually. (Courtesy Phoenix Zoo.)

The children's zoo was popular from the start. Here, in a photograph taken in the late 1960s, children play on one of the popular attractions of the children's zoo—the "shoe house" from the nursery rhyme about the old woman who lived in a shoe. (Courtesy Bauer family.)

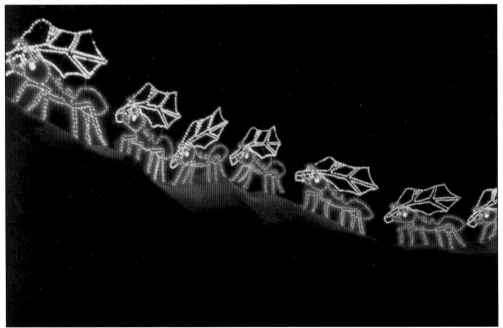

In December 1992, the Phoenix Zoo inaugurated Zoolights—extensive holiday lighting displays spread throughout the zoo for evening visitors to enjoy. Immensely popular, Zoolights is a major fund-raising event during the Christmas holiday season. In recent years, Zoolights has attracted nearly a quarter of a million people during its roughly 45-day run. (Courtesy Phoenix Zoo.)

Zoolights is not the only popular holiday activity within Papago Park. In 1978, the Desert Botanical Garden began its Las Noches de las Luminarias as a one-night free event for the public featuring mariachi music and 1,000 luminarias lining the pathways. Luminarias, a Southwestern tradition with Mexican roots, are paper bags lit by candles. (Courtesy Library Archives, Desert Botanical Garden.)

Las Noches de Las Luminarias became so popular that the Desert Botanical Garden began using it as a major fund-raising event, gradually adding days and more entertainment. By the 1990s, the event was held over four evenings during one weekend and was sold out many months in advance. In recent years, the event has been expanded to 19 nights spread over several weekends. Many thousands of luminarias are lit every night, and nearly a dozen entertainers are stationed throughout the garden to delight visitors. It has become a signature event for the Desert Botanical Garden. (Courtesy Library Archives, Desert Botanical Garden.)

The ever-evolving plans for Papago Park envisioned a multifaceted recreational and cultural experience. It has hiking trails, picnic areas, a golf course, a zoo, a botanical garden, and museums. In the late 1980s, the City of Tempe donated land in Papago Park for a new museum for the Arizona Historical Society. (Courtesy Arizona Historical Society, No. 1989.150.02.)

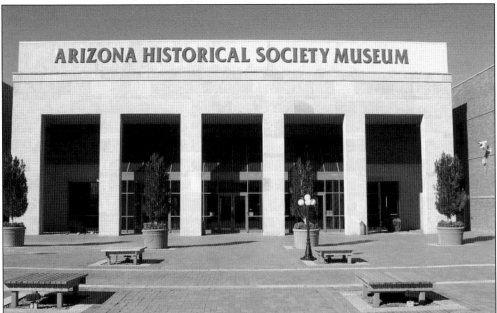

The Arizona Historical Society Museum opened in 1992 after several years of delays in securing necessary funds. The museum's extensive collection of historical artifacts and exhibits makes it popular with residents, tourists, and scholars. Of course, Papago Park will continue to evolve, but the original vision of a diversified pleasure park has been achieved. (Courtesy Hartz family.)

Two

SOUTH MOUNTAIN PARK/PRESERVE

South Mountain Park/Preserve has long been cited as the largest municipal park in the United States. By the early 1920s, Phoenix residents and community leaders knew that they wanted to protect what they then called the "Salt River Mountains" from increased mining activity and save them for recreational purposes. Although they would have liked to save the mountains for free through the federal government, their experiences with Papago Saguaro National Monument taught them that there was a significant price to pay in allowing federal control. So they decided that saving the Salt River Mountains was important enough to tax themselves to raise the funds to buy the land. Their foresight and initiative have given the Phoenix area the South Mountain Park/Preserve, more than 20 square miles of magnificent mountain and desert scenery, and have made it easily accessible for all to enjoy.

SOUTH MOUNTAIN PARK / PRESERVE

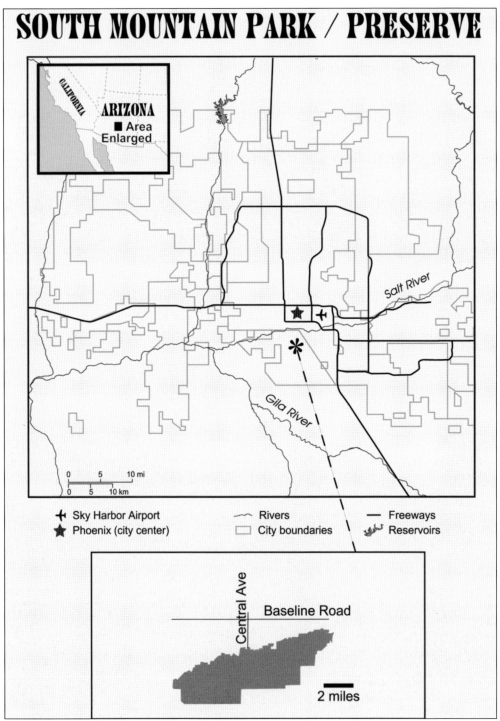

The 16,000 acres of South Mountain Park/Preserve are located in the southern part of Phoenix. It is most conveniently accessed via South Central Avenue, about seven miles south of downtown Phoenix. It has some 51 miles of major trails for hiking, biking, and horseback riding. (Map by Donna Hartz.)

The Salt River Mountains, as they were called prior to becoming a park, are located about seven miles south of Phoenix's city center. This 1915 photograph looking south down First Avenue shows the mountains in the distance. Although they did not contain any unique features like Papago Park's Buttes and Hole-in-the-Rock, the mountains still held considerable allure. (Courtesy McClintock Collection, Arizona Room, Phoenix Public Library.)

Although the Salt River Mountains may look similar to the untrained eye, the western portion is considerably older than the eastern portion of the mountain range. The western part of the mountains is metamorphic rock, created under extreme pressures and temperatures more than 1.7 billion years ago. The eastern end of the mountains is granite, an igneous rock formed only 25 million years ago when molten magma solidified below the earth's surface. (Courtesy Hartz family.)

The Salt River Mountain's geological makeup made them a good option for gold mining, with the first recorded mine dating from 1894. However, archeological evidence indicates that mining probably began as early as the Mexican era. By the 1910s, several dozen small mining efforts were under way, with optimistic talk about the possibility of extensive long-term mining. (Courtesy Hartz family.)

The mountains were a nearby place to escape the city—and to enjoy picnics, hikes, and magnificent views. Many groups took outings in the Salt River Mountains that included the challenge of arranging their members for a photograph, such as this one taken in 1920. (Courtesy McCulloch Brothers Photographs, Herb and Dorothy McLaughlin Collection, Arizona State University Libraries.)

The Salt River Mountains contained areas of great natural beauty, such as the one captured in this 1920s photograph of a magnificent saguaro cactus. It is easy to understand the value Phoenicians placed on these mountains and their growing concern that this place could be damaged by mining and development. (Courtesy McCulloch Brothers Photographs, Herb and Dorothy McLaughlin Collection, Arizona Sate University Libraries.)

James Dobbins, pictured above with his partner at one of his properties, was appointed in 1923 by the Phoenix Planning Commission to head a special committee charged to develop a plan to protect the Salt River Mountains from mining and development. Dobbins needed to move quickly, as the General Land Office survey had just been completed—the necessary step prior to opening the mountain acreage for disposal (sale). The subcommittee's first effort was a meeting with Carl Hayden to see if the land could be proclaimed a national monument, thereby becoming protected for free. However, the Department of Interior was not interested in that approach. (Courtesy Herb and Dorothy McLaughlin Collection, Arizona Sate University Libraries.)

Courtesy Phoenix Newspapers, Inc., Arizona Republican, April 6, 1924.

Dobbin's subcommittee eventually recommended to the Phoenix City Commission that Phoenix attempt to purchase some 14,500 acres from the federal government at a cost of $1.25 per acre. On April 4, 1924, the city commission approved Dobbins's plan. The news was spread via the *Arizona Republican* newspaper—with the promise of a "pleasure resort" for Phoenix's residents and winter visitors. (Courtesy Phoenix Newspapers, Inc., *Arizona Republican*, April 6, 1924.)

The plan to purchase the acreage was widely supported in Washington, D.C. On April 23, 1924, Pres. Calvin Coolidge, pictured, issued an executive order withdrawing the land from public acquisition pending necessary legislation. Congress passed the legislation June 7, 1924, and on October 1, of that year, the Phoenix City Commission authorized the payment of $18,124.47 for 14,513.98 acres. This created South Mountain Park, which has been long proclaimed as the nation's largest municipal park. (Courtesy Library of Congress.)

However, turning South Mountain Park into the promised "pleasure resort" was no easy task. Its mountainous nature made amenities, such as a swimming pool, fishing lake, golf course, etc., prohibitively expensive for the small city. Fortunately, some of the solution came from Pres. Franklin D. Roosevelt and his creation of the Civilian Conservation Corps (CCC). In this photograph, Roosevelt is surrounded by CCC workers. (Courtesy Carl T. Hayden Photographs, Arizona Collection, Arizona State University Libraries.)

The legislation to establish the CCC was passed with broad bipartisan support on March 31, 1933. It was immediately recognized by every state as an opportunity to put young men to work and as a way to accomplish many important infrastructure projects. Arizona secured a number of CCC companies, and Camp SP-4-A (pictured) was established in South Mountain Park. (Courtesy National Association of Civilian Conservation Corps Alumni, Chapter 44.)

The photographs to the left were a part of the 1936 annual report for CCC Company 2860, stationed at South Mountain Park. The report boasts that the "work of the company and those that have preceded it have made South Mountain Park much more useful as a rough mountain playground." It was certainly more accurate to be talking about a "rough mountain playground" than a "pleasure resort." The CCC was not only improving public spaces in Arizona, but also teaching its young workers. Those working at South Mountain Park had learned "jack hammer and compressor operation, truck driving, landscaping, surveying, and archeological excavation," as well as "handicraft in wood and metal." The CCC workers were invaluable in the creation of South Mountain Park and in fulfilling the 1924 dreams of James Dobbins and others. (Courtesy National Association of Civilian Conservation Corps Alumni, Chapter 44.)

South Mountain Park remained a popular place for picnics and excursions throughout the CCC years. This photograph from 1935 is of Ruth and Fred Wilson and friends on an excursion to South Mountain Park. An important benefit of the CCC activities was significantly improved automobile access. (Courtesy Fred Wilson Collection, Arizona Collection, Arizona State University Libraries.)

Another 1935 picture from Ruth and Fred Wilson showcases some of the improved picnic facilities. The CCC reported that one of the challenges of the South Mountain camp was ensuring pleasant experiences throughout the construction effort for the thousands of visitors who came to the park each year. (Courtesy Fred Wilson Collection, Arizona Collection, Arizona State University Libraries.)

The major priorities of the CCC within South Mountain Park were the construction of picnic grounds, ramadas, rest rooms, a corral, and a stable, as well as road and trail improvements. As can be seen from this photograph, the ramadas were beautiful as well as functional. (Courtesy Phoenix Parks and Recreation Department.)

During the 1930s, the CCC and the City of Phoenix built a number of view-point shelters, more than a dozen and a half ramadas, and more than 100 fire pits. An earlier hazardous road built by convict labor was improved and greatly expanded, allowing access to previously inaccessible portions of the park. (Courtesy Phoenix Parks and Recreation Department.)

One of the most important CCC improvements was expanded access to water. This photograph shows a CCC-built well over 100 feet deep. From the well, water was piped to some 30 water faucets throughout the park. (Courtesy Phoenix Parks and Recreation Department.)

The CCC also found itself involved in a variety of archeological activities within the park. The construction and road-building projects routinely uncovered archeological sites, including petroglyphs. This photograph shows an exhibit area built by the CCC to display some of the petroglyphs. (Courtesy Phoenix Parks and Recreation Department.)

Professional archeologists have long known that South Mountain Park contained a rich history of archeological sites. Most are between 600 and 1,300 years old and were produced by Hohokam and archaic people. This photograph shows a study of one such South Mountain Park site. (Courtesy Arizona Historical Foundation, Warren Krause Photograph Collection, No. KR-33.)

More than 8,000 petroglyph sites have been catalogued within South Mountain Park. This photograph shows the incredible beauty and complexity of these petroglyphs. This site has been nicknamed "newspaper rock." (Courtesy Arizona Historical Foundation, Warren Krause Photograph Collection, No. KR-34.)

The efforts of the CCC and the City of Phoenix may not have produced the originally envisioned "pleasure resort," but their foresight and efforts have preserved one of the Phoenix area's great treasures. In this 1959 photograph, a family enjoys the fruits of that effort and the wonders of the magnificent views. (Courtesy Bauer family.)

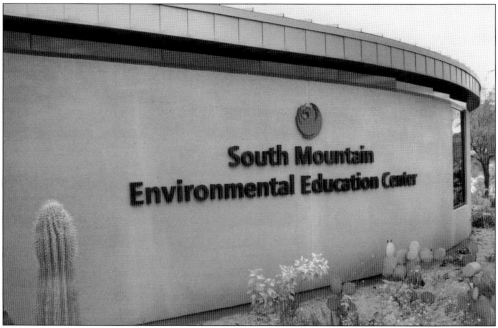

During the 1930s, more than $1 million was spent to create South Mountain Park. In 1939, the Phoenix Superintendent of Parks bragged that they intended to "operate this park as nearly like a national park as possible." This preservation mentality caused Phoenix to eventually add the title "Preserve" to the park's name and to open the "South Mountain Environmental Education Center" to educate visitors on the wonders of South Mountain and the importance of its preservation. (Courtesy Hartz family.)

Three

ENCANTO PARK

Phoenix community leaders had long recognized the need to provide residents and visitors with pleasure parks with extensive recreational amenities. Other western cities had built such parks, and Phoenix had aspirations to be a great city. Their experiences with South Mountain Park taught them that it was neither easy nor economical to build a pleasure park among the rugged mountains miles from the city center. Perhaps it would make more sense to build a great park from scratch on vacant and flat land closer to their residential districts. The story of Encanto Park is the story of the effort to build such a great pleasure park—with boating, golfing, picnicking, concerts, etc. With its creation, the quest for a great pleasure park would be achieved.

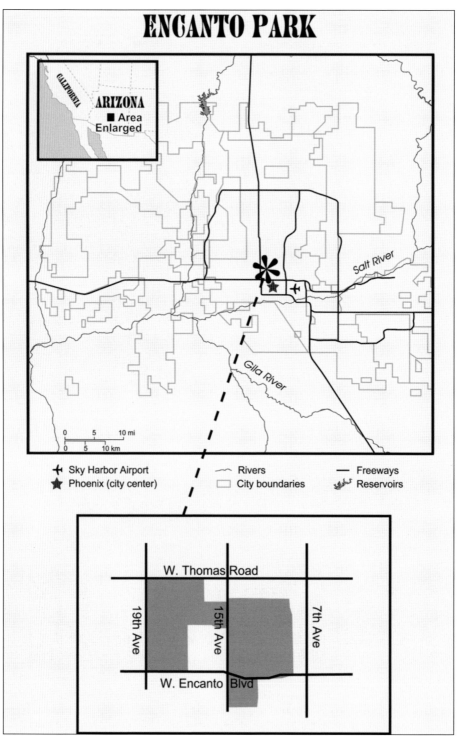

ENCANTO PARK

Legend:
- Sky Harbor Airport
- Phoenix (city center)
- Rivers
- City boundaries
- Freeways
- Reservoirs

Encanto Park is located about two miles north of downtown Phoenix and about a mile and a half west of North Central Avenue. Its main entrances are on Fifteenth Avenue south of Thomas Road and on Encanto Boulevard between Seventh and Fifteenth Avenues. (Map by Donna Hartz.)

By the late 1920s, residential development was occurring in the northern part of the city of Phoenix. In 1926, Dwight Heard, pictured, and his partner William Hartranft purchased 80 acres north of McDowell Road between Seventh and Fifteenth Avenues for a subdivision they named Palmcroft. Two years later, Lloyd Larkin and George Peter filed plat plans for the Encanto subdivision—just to the north of Palmcroft. Both were designed as higher-end subdivisions, creating a need for additional amenities in the area. (Courtesy Portrait Biography Collection, Arizona Collection, Arizona State University Libraries.)

In 1933, the Phoenix Parks and Recreation Board was created and William Hartranft was named its first president. Hartranft had long been intrigued by Balboa and Golden Gate Parks in California and wished to bring a world-class pleasure park to Phoenix. Putting it near his Palmcroft subdivision must have made great sense. In 1934, with a $900,000 grant from the federal Works Progress Administration (WPA), Hartranft began acquiring property for the new park—200-plus acres from the adjacent Dorris and Norton properties and approximately 20 acres from the Encanto subdivision. The Norton family house, pictured above during that era, later became the headquarters for the Phoenix Parks Department. (Courtesy Phoenix Museum of History.)

Like the neighboring subdivision, the park was named Encanto—which is also appropriately the Spanish word for enchantment—the perfect name given Hartranft's vision for Encanto Park. The park was designed by Hartranft with assistance from the WPA, and its construction between 1935 and 1938 was supervised by the WPA. Given the desert surroundings, water would be an important feature of the park. This 1939 photograph shows the result of that focus. (Courtesy Arizona Historical Foundation, Warren Krause Photograph Collection, No. KR-394.)

The boating lagoon at Encanto Park was over 2 miles long and was one of the most popular recreational features at the park—particularly boating by moonlight. This 1940 photograph shows the beauty of the boating experience, a special treat in the middle of the desert. (Courtesy Arizona Historical Foundation, Warren Krause Photograph Collection, No. KR-395.)

Another important goal for Encanto Park was to provide venues for a wide range of cultural activities. Early on, the large band shell became an important feature of the park, as can be seen from this 1940 photograph. (Courtesy Library of Congress.)

The band shell remained a centerpiece of Encanto Park for many decades, particularly for evening and weekend concerts and performances. It no longer survives but remained very popular into the late 1950s and early 1960s, as can be seen in the above photograph. (Courtesy Phoenix Parks and Recreation Department.)

One of the important early structures that still remains is the clubhouse, an elegant two-story building near the park's Fifteenth Avenue entrance. This 1949 photograph shows its attractive landscaping and Spanish design. The clubhouse initially served as a public restaurant. (Courtesy Phoenix Parks and Recreation Department.)

Another important early structure was the public boathouse, as seen in this 1949 photograph. The public could rent motorboats, canoes, and paddleboats from which they could enjoy the beautiful lagoons, the water birds, and the lush vegetation. (Courtesy Phoenix Parks and Recreation Department.)

Along with the cultural and boating activities, another priority for a proper pleasure park was extensive children's play facilities. This could be as simple as plenty of space to run around and sandboxes to play in. This 1949 photograph shows children enjoying an Encanto Park sandbox. (Courtesy Phoenix Parks and Recreation Department.)

In 1948, the voters of Phoenix approved a bond issue to finance park improvements. Among the early improvements at Encanto Park was the opening of a more elaborate amusement-park facility named Kiddieland. This 1949 photograph shows children enjoying the roller coaster at Kiddieland. (Courtesy Phoenix Parks and Recreation Department.)

Encanto Park was also designed to showcase vegetation, both native and lush oasis styles. A great deal of attention was always been paid to the landscaping at the park, including trees, shrubs, and flowers. This 1949 photograph showcases the lush oasis landscaping. (Courtesy Phoenix Parks and Recreation Department.)

Encanto Park was located in a desert environment, and eventually a beautiful cactus garden was included as a part of the landscaping plan. This photograph from 1960 shows a portion of the Encanto Park cactus garden. (Courtesy Phoenix Parks and Recreation Department.)

A public golf course was a key part of the Encanto Park design and was completed in the late 1930s. This 1950 photograph shows a view of the golf course from across the lagoon, with Squaw Peak in the distance. Undoubtedly, such spectacular vistas were a big part of the golf course's appeal. (Courtesy Arizona Historical Foundation, Warren Krause Photograph Collection, No. KR-397.)

It was also a challenging course for serious golfers. It was more than 6,000 yards in length and formed parts of the northern and eastern boundaries of the park. This 1954 photograph shows one of the larger sand hazards. (Courtesy Phoenix Parks and Recreation Department.)

Bond issues and capital budget increases allowed Phoenix to continually improve and upgrade the facilities at Encanto Park. Particularly important was continuing enhancement of the water features and the ability of the public to enjoy the water. This 1956 photograph shows workers constructing a new bridge across the lagoon. (Courtesy Phoenix Parks and Recreation Department.)

We get to see the results of that construction activity in this 1972 photograph of the very same lagoon bridge. The waterways of Encanto Park seem to be just as popular in 1972 as they were when it opened in the late 1930s. (Courtesy Phoenix Parks and Recreation Department.)

As the years went by, Kiddieland became more elaborate with a wider range of amusement rides. As would be typical of many small amusement parks, it frequently looked as if it could use some updating, but it remained very popular with families throughout the Phoenix area. (Courtesy Phoenix Parks and Recreation Department.)

One of the most popular features of Kiddieland was the steam train. The train carried visitors of all ages around Kiddieland and also along some of the lagoons, providing exciting views along the way. (Courtesy Phoenix Parks and Recreation Department.)

Encanto Park has always been synonymous with water fun. As can be seen from the above photograph, sections of the lagoon area were open for splashing and playing by the children, a perfect escape on those hot summer days. (Courtesy Phoenix Parks and Recreation Department.)

By the early 1980s, when the above photograph was taken, one could no longer rent motorboats for use on Encanto Park's lagoons. Instead paddleboats had become the water vehicle of choice and remained extremely popular with visitors to the park. (Courtesy Hartz family.)

Maintaining the appearance of a park as large and varied as Encanto Park requires significant expenditures, particularly as the facilities and vegetation age. Given competing needs for funds within the Phoenix parks system, the landscaping at Encanto has at times suffered despite the best efforts of the park's workers. (Courtesy Phoenix Parks and Recreation Department.)

This aerial of Encanto Park, probably from the 1960s, shows Kiddieland in the middle, a portion of the lagoon system surrounding Kiddieland and some of the picnic areas, and the golf course in the upper portion of the photograph. The band shell survives in the lower right corner. (Courtesy Phoenix Parks and Recreation Department.)

By the late 1980s, Kiddieland and many of its rides needed renovation or modernization. Times and technology were changing, and Kiddieland's popularity was declining. It was reborn in 1991 under the new name "Enchanted Island," containing many of the old favorites nicely refurbished and a new selection of rides and attractions. (Courtesy Hartz family.)

One of the old favorites is the Allan Herschell Carousel. Donated to Encanto Park in 1948, it was closed for renovation in the late 1980s. Lovingly restored to its former glory, it reopened in 1991. William Hartranft's vision of a first-class pleasure park has beautifully succeeded at Encanto Park over the past 70 years. Four generations of the authors' family have enjoyed the enchantment of Encanto Park and continue to do so through today. (Courtesy Hartz family.)

Four

ESTRELLA MOUNTAIN REGIONAL PARK

Estrella Mountain Regional Park might not immediately come to mind when preparing a list of the major parks and preserves in the Phoenix area. It does not have a signature mountain peak, such as Squaw Peak or Camelback Mountain. It does not have the extensive recreational facilities of Papago Park or Encanto Park or the magnificent mountain ridge road of South Mountain. Perhaps these are the reasons why one cannot find interesting pictures of residents or tourists picnicking in the area 100 years ago. However, it belongs on the list, both for its own important qualities and for what it represents—Estrella Mountain Regional Park was the first of the collection of magnificent Maricopa County mountain parks ringing the Valley of the Sun. It is an important story in the history of open space preservation within the Phoenix area.

ESTRELLA MOUNTAIN PARK

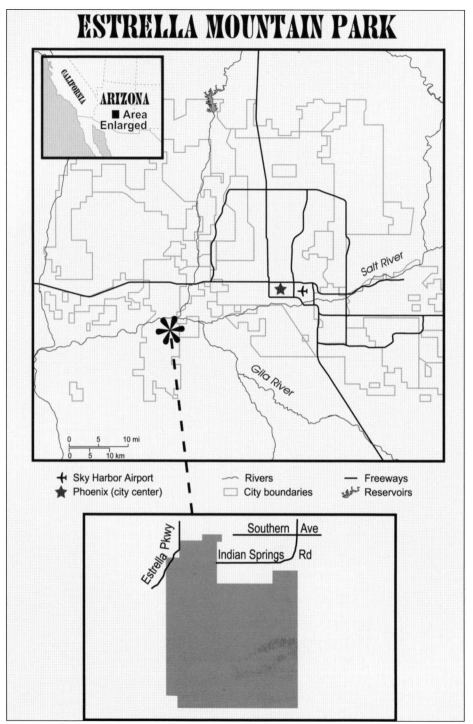

Estrella Mountain Regional Park is located in the city of Goodyear, a southwestern suburb of Phoenix. It is most conveniently reached by taking Estrella Parkway south from Interstate 10. Within the park's nearly 30 square miles are 27 miles of trails and a wide range of recreational facilities. (Map by Donna Hartz.)

This photograph, taken in the late 1920s, shows the Estrella Mountains from across the Gila River. The original Spanish language name, Sierra Estrella, means Star Mountains. Today we refer to this range as the Estrella Mountains, combining part of the Spanish name with part of the English translation. (Courtesy Arizona Historical Society, No. 1983.45.1317.)

This aerial photograph, probably taken in the early 1960s, shows some of the early site-preparation activity for the future park. Since the Estrella Mountains are south of the Gila River, they would have been part of Mexico after the Treaty of Guadalupe Hidalgo concluded the Mexican War. The Gadsden Purchase of 1854 moved the border south to its current position, placing the future park in the United States. (Courtesy Estrella Mountain Regional Park.)

In March 1953, the Maricopa County Parks Commission was created with Robert Jaap, pictured at left, as its first chairman. In the early 1950s, the vast majority of the land in the Phoenix area was unincorporated county property, giving Maricopa County the opportunity to be the prime mover in the effort to create parks and preserves. (Courtesy Herb and Dorothy McLaughlin Collection, Arizona State University Libraries.)

A significant amount of postwar industrial and residential growth was occurring in the western part of the Phoenix area. Community leaders began lobbying for the creation of parks and other recreational amenities in the west valley to meet the needs of the growing population. In November 1953, the Maricopa County Parks Commission purchased 250 acres adjoining the Estrella Mountains for $2,500, and accepted the assignment of a lease for an additional 400 acres from the state for $25 per year. This aerial photograph looks down over this parkland. (Courtesy Estrella Mountain Regional Park.)

As always, acquiring the land was the easy part; the challenge was securing funding to build the recreational facilities. Estrella Mountain Park received an initial budget of about $9,000 for ramadas, fireplaces, rest rooms, a water well, and a softball diamond. Volunteer help was very important, as seen in this late-1950s photograph of Boy Scouts at work. (Courtesy Estrella Mountain Regional Park.)

While the county funded improvements requiring specialized construction expertise and equipment, the Boy Scouts focused on trail building, as the park was intended to include many miles of hiking trails. (Courtesy Estrella Mountain Regional Park.)

The Maricopa County Parks Commission decided from the beginning that Estrella Mountain Park would have extensive recreational facilities to rival the parks in Phoenix. A key element of that plan was inclusion of a golf course. This photograph from the early 1960s shows the future site of the golf course. (Courtesy Estrella Mountain Regional Park.)

The official ground-breaking ceremony for the Estrella Mountain Park Golf Course involved a first tee shot, rather than a shovel full of dirt, with the earth-moving equipment in the background of this picture from the early 1960s. (Courtesy Estrella Mountain Regional Park.)

The photograph shows another view of the golf course during the final stages of construction as well as a surveyor ensuring that everything was lined up perfectly to provide a challenging course for the golfers. (Courtesy Estrella Mountain Regional Park.)

The golf course required a pro shop, and this photograph shows a team of workers busily involved in the framing. The golf course opened in 1964. (Courtesy Estrella Mountain Regional Park.)

County parks planners decided that a 65-acre portion of Estrella Mountain Regional Park would be developed for what they called "active recreation." This area, known as the Casey Abbott Semi-Regional Park was officially opened on April 19, 1964. (Courtesy Estrella Mountain Regional Park.)

Casey Abbott was the longtime chairman of the Maricopa County Planning Commission and was a strong supporter of the development of parks and the preservation of the Phoenix area's spectacular desert and mountain scenery. This 1941 photograph shows Casey Abbott and his two dogs. (Courtesy Sen. Carl Hayden Photographs, Arizona Collection, Arizona State University Libraries.)

Obviously the heart of any "active recreation" area would have to include a good collection of playground equipment for children. Clearly there was plenty of active recreation on opening day in 1964. (Courtesy Estrella Mountain Regional Park.)

As can be seen in the background of these opening day photographs of children at the playground, the initial landscaping was rather sparse. But the immediate priority was the creation of the play area for the children; the landscaping could come later. (Courtesy Estrella Mountain Regional Park.)

Another facility in place for the April 1964 opening of the Casey Abbott Semi-Regional Park was the large amphitheater. This would be a popular site for future performances, meetings, and other events. (Courtesy Estrella Mountain Regional Park.)

Eventually the active recreation area was renamed the Casey Abbott Recreation Area and included the golf course, playground, picnic area with ramadas, the amphitheater, and a rodeo arena. All have remained in active use through today. (Courtesy Hartz family.)

Under the leadership of Jaap and Abbott, Maricopa County developed a vision of a series of regional mountain parks surrounding the Phoenix area preserving the spectacular desert and mountain scenery. Estrella Mountain was the first, but it was quickly followed by several others in the 1950s. One other important example is the White Tank Mountain Regional Park, pictured here, which is the largest member of the county park system. (Courtesy Hartz family.)

Located on the western edge of the Valley of the Sun, White Tank Mountain Regional Park is nearly 30,000 acres in size and has peaks reaching 4,000 feet. It gets its name from depressions or "tanks" formed by erosion in the white granite rocks of the mountain range. (Courtesy Hartz family.)

In addition to the spectacular scenery, the White Tanks are known for their amazing collection of petroglyph sites. The Hohokam occupied 11 archeological sites in the White Tanks between 500 and 1,100 A.D. Most of the petroglyph sites can be attributed to the Hohokam, but some sites may approach 10,000 years in age. (Courtesy Arizona Historical Foundation, Warren Krause Photograph Collection, No. KR-31.)

Obviously these photographs from over 50 years ago do not portray professional archeologists, nor currently accepted visitor behavior. But the petroglyphs have proven to be very popular with park visitors and are easily accessible via a short trail to Petroglyph Plaza. (Courtesy Arizona Historical Foundation, Warren Krause Photograph Collection, No. KR-32.)

The huge regional parks assembled by Maricopa County in the 1950s and 1960s, including Estrella and White Tanks, were mostly made up of land leased to the county by the federal government. In addition to the continuing costs of the lease, the land use limitations restricted the county's ability to improve many of the park amenities. Arizona's Stewart Udall, pictured, while secretary of the interior from 1961 through 1969, was extremely helpful in the purchase of the leased land. He set a highly attractive price of $2.50 per acre for the county to purchase this land. (Courtesy Arizona Historical Foundation, Biography Subject Photograph Collection, No. B-77.)

Democratic senator and former governor Paul Fannin, pictured above at a softball game between his staff and Barry Goldwater's staff, also knew how to play legislative hardball. He led the Congressional effort to enact legislation authorizing Maricopa County to buy 68,110 acres at Udall's attractive pricing. On October 21, 1970, the bill was signed into law by President Nixon, and the county's massive regional park system became a reality, including 17,113 acres for the park that started it all—Estrella Mountain Regional Park. (Courtesy Arizona Historical Foundation, Robert Creighton Photograph Collection, No. CRE-238.)

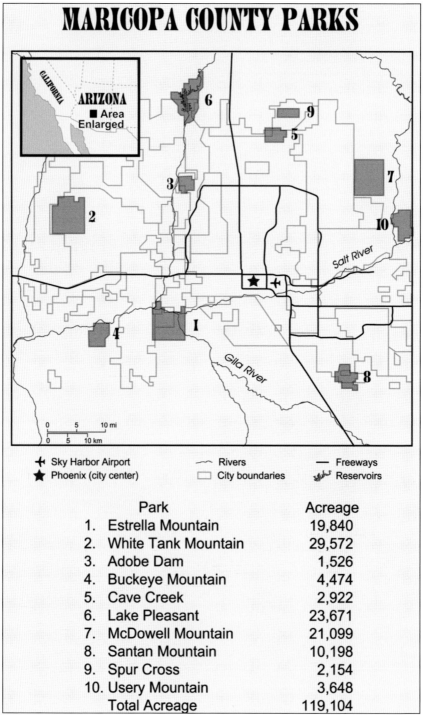

MARICOPA COUNTY PARKS

Park	Acreage
1. Estrella Mountain	19,840
2. White Tank Mountain	29,572
3. Adobe Dam	1,526
4. Buckeye Mountain	4,474
5. Cave Creek	2,922
6. Lake Pleasant	23,671
7. McDowell Mountain	21,099
8. Santan Mountain	10,198
9. Spur Cross	2,154
10. Usery Mountain	3,648
Total Acreage	119,104

Maricopa County has built a ring of desert and mountain parks that surround the Valley of the Sun and preserve some of the Phoenix area's most spectacular mountain and desert scenery. Encompassing some 180 square miles, the Maricopa County park system is one of the Phoenix area's greatest assets. (Map by Donna Hartz.)

Five

CAMELBACK MOUNTAIN

Camelback Mountain is perhaps the most recognizable mountain within the Phoenix area. All of its land was privately owned, so its preservation was both a special challenge and a special imperative. In the 1950s and 1960s, there were serious development plans to put a revolving restaurant on the top of the camel's hump and erect a cable car system to bring diners and tourists to the summit. Even though those plans would never materialize, technology was allowing homes to be built higher on the mountain on much steeper slopes. The story of the preservation of Camelback Mountain is the story of ordinary people and community leaders rising up in a near emergency situation and putting their money where their mouth was to stop the development and preserve this natural treasure.

CAMELBACK MOUNTAIN

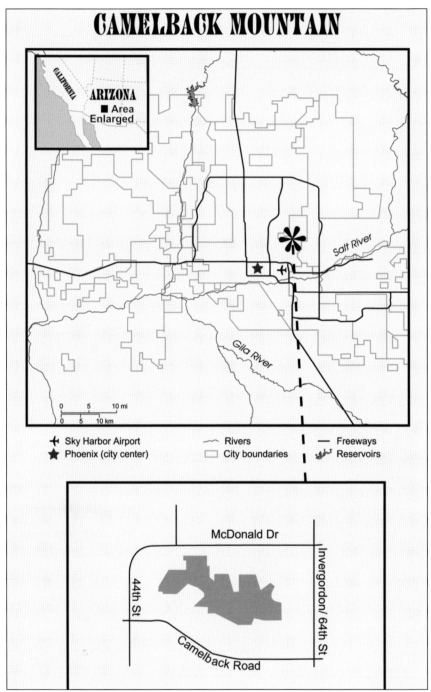

Camelback Mountain is located in Phoenix between Camelback Road and McDonald Drive, roughly halfway between SR51 and SR101. The park is almost completely surrounded by private property. However, there is public access from both the west and the east. The most convenient access is from the west via the Echo Canyon Recreation area, just east of Tatum Boulevard off of McDonald Drive. The summit can also be reached via the Cholla Trail, with limited street parking on Invergordon/Sixty-fourth Street at Cholla Lane. (Map by Donna Hartz.)

Camelback Mountain is perhaps the best known and most easily recognizable natural feature within the Phoenix area. It towers some 1,500 feet above the surrounding desert floor (summit elevation is 2,704 feet above sea level) and extends about 2 miles east to west and about 1 mile north to south. Geologically the mountain is really in two parts. The huge camel's back is a mass of granite approximately 1.5 billion years old. The camel's head at the western portion of the mountain is sedimentary rock, mostly sandstone, laid down within the past 100 million years. (Courtesy Arizona Historical Foundation, Warren Krause Photograph Collection, No. KR-392.)

The photographs on this page were from the first decades of the 20th century; the first view from the south, and the second from the north. During the last decade of the 19th century, the area around Camelback was surveyed by the federal government and made available for private acquisition. Up until the 1930s, the mountain was variously referred to as "Camel Back," "Camelsback," and "Camelback." (Courtesy Scottsdale Public Library's Southwest Collection.)

Development pressure in the Camelback area began fairly early thanks to W. J. Murphy. In the 1880s, Murphy built the Arizona Canal, running some 50 miles from the Salt River just below the junction with the Verde River to New River, with an alignment just south of Camelback Mountain. This construction photograph from the early 1880s shows Camelback Mountain in the background. (Courtesy Library of Congress.)

Murphy built a dirt access road adjacent to the canal, greatly increasing public accessibility to the Camelback area. This photograph, taken around the start of the 20th century, shows the canal road with Camelback Mountain in the background. (Courtesy Arizona Historical Foundation, Robert Creighton Photograph Collection, No. CRE-274.)

The Arizona Canal itself quickly became quite a recreational attraction, particularly in the area immediately south of Camelback Mountain. At that point the caliche rock became such a challenge for the canal excavators that a waterfall was created. Arizona Falls, as it was called, dropped nearly 20 feet and immediately became a major tourist attraction. This photograph from the first decade of the 20th century shows Arizona Falls in all of its glory. (Courtesy Scottsdale Public Library's Southwest Collection.)

The Arizona Canal was also an obstacle that needed to be bridged, if only for pedestrian crossing. This early-20th-century photograph shows a rope and plank bridge crossing the canal, probably from the village of Scottsdale, again with Camelback Mountain in the background. (Courtesy Scottsdale Public Library's Southwest Collection.)

Camelback Mountain dominated the views throughout the Phoenix area, and the improved accessibility via the canal road was an irresistible urge to many residents and tourists. This photograph from 1900 shows the classic view of Camelback. (Courtesy Arizona Historical Foundation, Robert Creighton Photograph Collection, No. CRE-216.)

Camelback Mountain was only about 10 miles from downtown Phoenix. This photograph looking northeast from central Phoenix about 1900 shows Camelback dominating the skyline. (Courtesy Arizona Historical Foundation, Robert Creighton Photograph Collection, No. CRE-80.)

W. J. Murphy was a smart businessman and quickly appreciated the impact of the canal he was building on land values. He acquired large tracts of land along the canal and experimented with a wide range of agricultural products. He realized that the land adjacent to Arizona Falls, and just south of Camelback Mountain, could be particularly valuable. It was developed into the site of his Ingleside Club, shown under construction in this 1909 photograph. (Courtesy Scottsdale Public Library's Southwest Collection.)

Ingleside became the Phoenix area's first major resort and a major attraction for winter visitors. The club was closed during the hot summer months. This photograph from the 1910s shows Ingleside and its landmark tower, with Camelback Mountain in the background. (Courtesy Arizona Historical Foundation, Robert Creighton Photograph Collection, No. CRE-282.)

Murphy built a golf course for Ingleside Club guests along the canal. The greens were oiled sand rather than grass, providing an interesting challenge to the golfer in this early-20th-century photograph. (Courtesy Scottsdale Historical Society.)

Ingleside Club was eventually renamed Ingleside Inn, and it was instrumental in focusing attention on the Camelback Mountain area for both local residents and tourists. This photograph shows the main gate of the Ingleside Inn in the 1920s. (Courtesy Scottsdale Historical Society.)

Murphy and his son made extensive use of Camelback Mountain area to provide their guests with Old West experiences. Elaborate banquets were held in Echo Canyon, on the northern side of the camel's head. This photograph from the 1920s shows one such banquet. (Courtesy Scottsdale Historical Society.)

The tourists attending these banquets expected Native American entertainment, and expected the Native Americans to look like the ones in the movies. So Ingleside's Native American entertainers wore the headdresses of the northern plains Native American. Ingleside Inn also used Camelback Mountain for excursions, and members of its staff built the first trail to the summit. (Courtesy Scottsdale Historical Society.)

Local residents also felt the allure of Camelback Mountain, and it was a popular location for day trips and picnics. This photograph from 1910 shows a group enjoying Camelback Mountain after a horse-drawn carriage ride. (Courtesy Herb and Dorothy McLaughlin Collection, Arizona State University Libraries.)

The Luhrs, a prominent Phoenix family, frequently brought their camera on their various excursions. This Luhrs family photograph from 1913 shows a finely dressed group at Camelback who, after arriving by automobile, has set up a picnic to enjoy. (Courtesy Luhrs Family Photographs, Arizona Collection, Arizona State University Libraries.)

The Luhrs also enjoyed much less formal trips to Camelback Mountain. In this 1913 family photograph, four girls climb a pole—perhaps for a better view, but most definitely for a memorable photograph. (Courtesy Luhrs Family Photographs, Arizona Collection, Arizona State University Libraries.)

This 1916 Luhrs family photograph shows five people seated on a rocky ledge in the Echo Canyon area of Camelback Mountain and dressed in a variety of styles for their Camelback excursion. (Courtesy Luhrs Family Photographs, Arizona Collection, Arizona State University Libraries.)

Climbing the rocks of Camelback Mountain was a popular pastime for young and old alike. This 1920s photograph shows these Camelback Mountain hikers enjoying the spectacular views. (Courtesy Scottsdale Public Library's Southwest Collection.)

By the late 1920s, Camelback Mountain had become more easily accessible and was frequently the site of a wide range of events and activities. This photograph shows a multitude arriving for an Easter sunrise service at Camelback Mountain in the late 1920s. (Courtesy McCulloch Brothers Photographs, Herb and Dorothy McLaughlin Collection, Arizona State University Libraries.)

Despite the rapidly increasing influx of visitors, the Camelback Mountain area remained a place of great natural beauty. This 1929 photograph shows a large and spectacular saguaro cactus with Camelback Mountain in the background. Rapid development in the area during the first half of the 20th century would soon threaten significant portions of that natural beauty. (Courtesy Herb and Dorothy McLaughlin Collection, Arizona State University Libraries.)

The Arizona Canal opened up the area around Camelback Mountain for agriculture, and during the first decades of the 20th century, there was considerable crop experimentation. This photograph shows an attempt to create vineyards out of the desert. (Courtesy Library of Congress.)

Agricultural experiments with citrus groves, primarily oranges, in the Camelback Mountain area began as early as the late 1880s. Citrus quickly became the preferred crop, and the area to the south of Camelback contained thousands of acres of citrus. This photograph from 1932 shows one such citrus orchard. (Courtesy McCulloch Brothers Photographs, Herb and Dorothy McLaughlin Collection, Arizona State University Libraries.)

The beauty of the Camelback Mountain area was an important draw for tourists, and, not surprisingly, tourism entrepreneurs took notice. Ingleside Inn had fallen on hard times during the Depression, and the area was ripe for new resort alternatives. In the mid-1930s, the combination of Jack Stewart's resort expertise and John C. Lincoln's money gave the valley a premier resort—Camelback Inn, seen in this late-1930s photograph. (Courtesy Scottsdale Public Library's Southwest Collection.)

Camelback Inn opened in December 1936 and was an immediate success, combining luxury with an isolated, Western atmosphere. It was located on the north side of Camelback Mountain, 12 miles northeast of Phoenix. This photograph from the 1930s looks to the north with Mummy Mountain in the background. (Courtesy Scottsdale Public Library's Southwest Collection.)

Jack Stewart's goal for Camelback Inn was to provide his guests with a real Western experience—trail rides, picnics excursions, and an Old West feel to all of the facilities. There would also be extensive social opportunities for his wealthy guests, but the feel would always be Western. That image is exemplified in this Camelback Inn postcard from the 1940s. (Courtesy Scottsdale Historical Society.)

Camelback Mountain has always been a centerpiece of the Camelback Inn's Western experience. Guided hikes and horseback rides, as seen in this late 1930s photograph, focused on Camelback Mountain—in particular, the Echo Canyon area, only a short ride from the Camelback Inn. (Courtesy Scottsdale Public Library's Southwest Collection.)

The success of the Camelback Inn drew additional resort competitors to the Camelback Mountain area. One of the best and most successful was Jokake Inn, located up against Camelback Mountain on the south side. It was a small, exclusive facility with striking Western décor. This photograph from the 1940s shows the facade of the main building. (Courtesy Arizona Historical Foundation, Warren Krause Photograph Collection, No. KR-685.)

The grounds of Jokake Inn, as seen in this 1940s photograph, continued the Western theme, as did its excursions and social events. An important impact of the Camelback Inn and Jokake Inn was to showcase the attractiveness of a Camelback Mountain location to both wealthy Phoenicians as well as to winter visitors. Camelback Mountain became the place to build a home. (Courtesy Arizona Historical Foundation, Warren Krause Photograph Collection, No. KR-683)

This 1949 aerial photograph of Camelback Mountain looking to the northeast shows that immediately postwar it maintained its relatively isolated, undeveloped feel. Although all of the land was privately owned at this point, there are only the early signs of development up against the mountain. In fact, it was in 1949 that the first house was built on the mountain slope of the south side of Camelback Mountain. (Courtesy Herb and Dorothy McLaughlin Collection, Arizona State University Libraries.)

This 1954 aerial photograph of Camelback Mountain shows some fairly dramatic changes. Both the citrus orchards and the residential development are now close to the base of Camelback Mountain, with more signs of development on the mountainside. In 1954, Maricopa County Planning Commission chairman Casey Abbott warned of potential development on Camelback Mountain, and in that same year, the Camelback Improvement Association was founded with a goal to preserve the mountain in its natural state. (Courtesy Scottsdale Public Library's Southwest Collection.)

But the development continued. This 1957 aerial, looking to the northwest from Scottsdale, shows development now beginning to surround Camelback. A common goal of the preservationists was to prohibit development above the elevation of 1,600 feet above sea level. The County Planning Commission tried to block development, citing safety concerns; an Arizona legislator asked Congress to create a national monument above 1,600 feet; and the Phoenix Community Council considered a 1,600-foot resolution. However, the problem in all cases was that the land above 1,600 feet was privately owned. (Courtesy Scottsdale Public Library's Southwest Collection.)

Still the development continued. This 1970 aerial photograph shows homes pressed tightly against the mountain, as well as climbing up the sides—with ever-increasing excavations for new homes higher up the mountain. The views of the natural Camelback Mountain might have completely disappeared if not for the preservation activism of the 1960s. The initiatives came from many directions—wealthy garden club matrons like Gertrude Devine Webster who wanted to save their views, outdoor enthusiasts who wanted access to Camelback Mountain, schoolchildren roused to action by the *Arizona Republic* newspaper, etc. (Courtesy Herb and Dorothy McLaughlin Collection, Arizona State University Libraries.)

But extraordinary leadership was needed to make it happen. Barry Goldwater was the right leader, with the right cause, at the right time. Goldwater came from a prominent mercantile family with long and deep ties to Arizona. He was always an outdoors enthusiast with a great love for Arizona's natural treasures. In this photograph, a young Goldwater enjoys a hike in the desert. (Courtesy Arizona Historical Foundation, Barry Morris Goldwater Fine Arts Photograph Collection.)

By the mid-1960s it was apparent that raising money to buy the private land was the only way to preserve Camelback Mountain. After losing the 1964 presidential race, Barry Goldwater was out of the Senate and available to lead a cause in which he intensely believed. In November 1964, the Preservation of Camelback Mountain Foundation was formed, and Barry Goldwater, pictured above atop Camelback, was named chairman. (Courtesy Arizona Historical Foundation, Barry Morris Goldwater Fine Arts Photograph Collection.)

The vice-chair was Margaret Kober, pictured at right, who served on the Phoenix City Council with Goldwater in the early 1950s and knew how to get things done in Phoenix. The goal was to purchase the 352 acres above the 1,800 foot level, at an estimated cost of $555,000. By 1967, Kober and Goldwater had succeeded in raising $285,000, from both large and small contributions from citizens throughout the Phoenix area. (Courtesy Herb and Dorothy McLaughlin Collection, Arizona State University Libraries.)

Maricopa County, with the backing of the state, applied for a federal grant to make up the shortfall. Arizona native Stewart Udall was secretary of the interior—and available to help grease the skids—and on May 20, 1968, first lady Lady Bird Johnson presented a check for $211,250 at a gala event in Phoenix. The first lady and Barry Goldwater are pictured in this photograph from that evening. The money was now in hand to purchase and preserve all of Camelback Mountain above 1,800 feet. (Courtesy Arizona Historical Foundation, Barry Morris Goldwater Fine Arts Photograph Collection.)

But there was no plan to allow public access to Camelback Mountain. Gary Driggs, pictured, a local financier and a lifelong hiker and climber of Camelback, aggressively and creatively led a successful effort to ensure public access to Camelback from both the eastern and western sides. Driggs later wrote the definitive book about the mountain, *Camelback, Sacred Mountain of Phoenix*. (Courtesy Arizona Historical Foundation, Biography Subject Photograph Collection, No. B-910.)

Impending plans to develop the Echo Canyon area caught the attention of Driggs and others. It was felt that Echo Canyon, which showed evidence of sacred use by native groups, needed to be preserved for its history and also as the western access point to the mountain. Driggs's efforts eventually led to the preservation of Echo Canyon and its use as the primary access point for hikes and climbs up Camelback Mountain and throughout Echo Canyon. This photograph shows a portion of the access trail in Echo Canyon. Camelback Mountain was preserved because the people wanted it preserved—and because community leaders rose to the occasion and made it happen. (Courtesy Hartz family.)

Six

Squaw Peak and the Phoenix Mountains Preserve

The unique shape of Squaw Peak and its large size drew attention and visitors for as long as there have been people in the Phoenix area. Owing to its challenging climb and spectacular views, the hike to the top via the summit trail is claimed to be one of the most popular urban hikes in the United States. Although the peak itself had long been protected from development by state ownership, the mountains and hills surrounding it were ripe candidates for development. The early preservation activity surrounding Squaw Peak was first to ensure a properly sized park for the peak area itself, and then to feature it as a key component in an overall plan for a Phoenix Mountains Preserve. It should be noted that the name "Squaw Peak" is used when referring to the period in which it had that name, and the mountain's renaming as Piestewa Peak is celebrated in the honoring of a fallen hero.

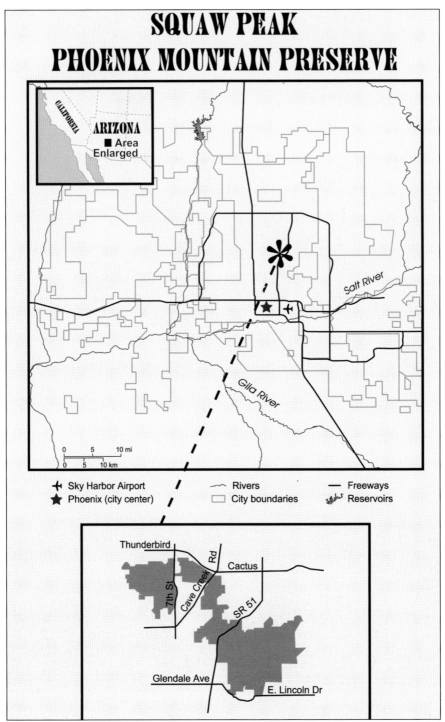

SQUAW PEAK
PHOENIX MOUNTAIN PRESERVE

The Phoenix Mountains Preserve, including Piestewa Peak (formerly known as Squaw Peak), is located in the central part of Phoenix and is pierced by SR51. The extremely popular Piestewa Peak Summit Trail is 1.2 miles in length, with a 1,200 foot elevation gain. Parking areas can be accessed via Squaw Peak Drive, off of Glendale Avenue east of SR51. (Map by Donna Hartz.)

The mountain that was historically called Squaw Peak is part of the Phoenix Mountains range, located about eight miles north of the original Phoenix town site. This photograph from the beginning of the 20th century shows a portion of the Phoenix Mountains, with Squaw Peak on the left. It is composed of metamorphic rock known as schist, and was elevated during the basin and range formation period about 14 million years ago. (Courtesy Arizona Historical Foundation, Gusse Thomas Smith Photograph Collection, No. GTS-46.)

In the vicinity of Squaw Peak, there is evidence of Hohokam settlement dating from the 1100–1450 A.D. period. Given the prominence of the peak, it is likely that there has been human activity around Squaw Peak for as long as there have been people in the valley. In the 1880s, the U.S. Army used Squaw Peak as a heliograph station. This early-20th-century photograph again features Squaw Peak as a part of the Phoenix Mountain range. (Courtesy Arizona Historical Foundation, Robert Creighton Photograph Collection, No. CRE-271.)

Similar to the case at Camelback Mountain, it was the building of the Arizona Canal in the 1880s that accelerated the arrival of tourism, agriculture, and development to the Squaw Peak area. This photograph from the 1910s shows a portion of the canal with Squaw Peak rising majestically in the background. (Courtesy Phoenix Parks and Recreation Department.)

This early-1920s view from the banks of the canal just south of Squaw Peak shows Camelback Mountain in the distance. The canal brought agriculture, residential settlement, and improved roads—making the Squaw Peak area more accessible to both residents and tourists. (Courtesy Arizona Historical Foundation, Gusse Thomas Smith Photograph Collection, No. GTS-53.)

The unique and prominent shape of Squaw Peak could be seen from all over the Phoenix area and attracted outdoor enthusiasts like a magnet. This photograph from the 1910s shows a group of such enthusiasts attempting to climb its rugged slopes. (Courtesy Phoenix Parks and Recreation Department.)

As was true throughout the Phoenix area, the early part of the 20th century saw a wide range of agricultural and ranching use in the Squaw Peak area. This photograph shows a herd of goats grazing on the land south of Squaw Peak. (Courtesy Scottsdale Public Library's Southwest Collection.)

Tourism was important at Squaw Peak throughout the 20th century, and the tourism industry attracted some very clever entrepreneurs. One very important example was the McArthur brothers who, among other achievements, created the "Wonderbus," pictured above in a photograph from around 1920. (Courtesy Arizona Historical Foundation, Gusse Thomas Smith Photograph Collection, No. GTS-40.)

Warren and Charles McArthur opened a dozen automobile dealerships in Arizona during the 1910s and adapted a Dodge truck to create Wonderbus, one of the earliest recreational vehicles. They carried tourists to elaborate picnics near Squaw Peak, as seen above, as well as on longer camping trips to view natural wonders throughout Arizona. (Courtesy Arizona Historical Foundation, Gusse Thomas Smith Photograph Collection, No. GTS-41.)

In addition to a well-equipped kitchen and various picnic paraphernalia and fold-down cots, the Wonderbus included the latest in seating comfort, as well as large picture windows to view the sights. Thanks to the McArthur brothers, lucky tourists were able to enjoy the Squaw Peak area from the comfort of the Wonderbus. (Courtesy Arizona Historical Foundation, Gusse Thomas Smith Photograph Collection, No. GTS-42.)

Other groups also flocked to the Phoenix Mountains and Squaw Peak. This photograph from the early 1920s shows what appears to be a large group of well-dressed businessmen awkwardly eating some sort of meal balanced on their laps. Who they are, how they got there, and why they do not have more comfortable dining arrangements remains a mystery. (Courtesy Arizona Historical Foundation, Gusse Thomas Smith Photograph Collection, No. GTS-45.)

There was another McArthur brother who was even more important to the story of Squaw Peak. Albert Chase McArthur was a former student of Frank Lloyd Wright and was hired by a group of investors, including brothers Warren and Charles, to design and build a magnificent resort at the foot of Squaw Peak. Frank Lloyd Wright consulted on the project and inspired the design, and the Arizona Biltmore hotel, seen above during construction, opened on February 23, 1929. (Courtesy Arizona Collection, Arizona State University Libraries.)

The Arizona Biltmore's spectacular design and setting made it an immediate success, and brought many of the rich and famous to the shadow of Squaw Peak. According to hotel brochures, Irving Berlin wrote his classic *White Christmas* while sitting poolside at the Arizona Biltmore hotel. (Courtesy Arizona Historical Foundation, Warren Krause Photograph Collection, No. KR-680.)

The Arizona Biltmore included a beautiful golf course among its many recreational amenities. This well-dressed "fivesome" is enjoying a round of golf at the Arizona Biltmore, with Squaw Peak in the background. (Courtesy Arizona Historical Foundation, Gusse Thomas Smith Photograph Collection, No. GTS-63.)

The Arizona Biltmore took advantage of its location alongside the Phoenix Mountains to offer horseback riding, as pictured here in the early 1930s, and hiking into the mountains. In fact, it was the staff of the Arizona Biltmore that improved the first public trail to the summit of Squaw Peak. (Courtesy Arizona Historical Foundation, Gusse Thomas Smith Photograph Collection, No. GTS-54.)

This photograph from the early 1930s looks east across the Biltmore's buildings toward Camelback Mountain in the distance. Following the tradition of the Ingleside Inn, the Arizona Biltmore brought Western hospitality and desert luxury to the tourism market, adding to the allure of the Phoenix area and promoting the magnificent mountain scenery. (Courtesy Library of Congress.)

This aerial photograph, taken shortly after the opening of the Arizona Biltmore, shows the extensiveness of the Biltmore's facilities and its relative isolation at the foot of the Phoenix Mountains. (Courtesy Arizona Historical Foundation, Gusse Thomas Smith Photograph Collection, No. GTS-48.)

The area south of the Arizona Biltmore remained mostly agricultural during the 1940s, as the war limited development activity in the Phoenix area. This photograph from the early 1950s, along the Arizona Canal, looking toward Squaw Peak, shows few signs of the extraordinary development that would occur in the Squaw Peak area over the next two decades. (Courtesy Library of Congress.)

This 1970 aerial photograph shows commercial and residential development pushing right up to the slopes of the Phoenix Mountains. Squaw Peak itself had been protected in 1958 when Maricopa County created Squaw Peak Park on 388 acres leased from the state. On July 1, 1960, the county turned Squaw Peak Park and nearby North Mountain Park over to the City of Phoenix. But development in the 1960s raised the real possibility that these parks would be isolated peaks in a sea of homes. (Courtesy Herb and Dorothy McLaughlin Collection, Arizona State University Libraries.)

An early advocate for the creation of a larger Phoenix Mountains Preserve encompassing Squaw Peak and North Mountain Parks was Dorothy Gilbert, pictured at left. Under her leadership in early 1966, petitions with more than 1,200 signatures were presented to the Phoenix City Council calling for a moratorium on development in the Phoenix Mountains area and the development of a comprehensive preservation plan. On August 6, 1966, the Phoenix City Council unanimously adopted a plan to preserve the open space character of the area. (Courtesy Herb and Dorothy McLaughlin Collection, Arizona State University Libraries.)

A slightly expanded Squaw Peak Park was dedicated in November 1968, and in 1969, an additional 162 acres of Bureau of Land Management (BLM) land was acquired for Squaw Peak and North Mountain Parks. By 1970, Squaw Peak Park had been expanded to 546 acres, and the Phoenix Mountains Preservation Council was founded with the objective of "setting aside the Phoenix Mountains as a unique wilderness park." By 1972, the Phoenix City Council approved the "Open Space Plan For The Phoenix Mountains," pictured at right, to preserve 9,711 acres within the Phoenix Mountains. (Courtesy Dorothy Gilbert Papers, Arizona Collection, Arizona State University Libraries.)

GIVE YOURSELF A FUTURE

Give them a place to play

Provide them an
opportunity to explore

Save, for them, our land's natural beauty

Protect them, by preparing our
Emergency Services

VOTE YES ON JUNE 5TH — PHOENIX IS IN YOUR HANDS

During the 1970s and 1980s, a series of bond issues were presented to the Phoenix voters to fund acquisition of land for the preserve. Most passed, showing the widespread support for preserving the Phoenix Mountains. This mailer from 1984 is typical of the message promoting preservation. (Courtesy Dorothy Gilbert Papers, Arizona Collection, Arizona State University Libraries.)

The successful effort to create the Phoenix Mountains Preserve also required a series of electoral and legislative victories. In May 1972, Arizona voters approved a constitutional amendment to allow bonding for park and open space acquisition expenditures. In 1990, the state legislature passed House Bill 2218, requiring consent of local voters before any highway could be constructed through the preserve. Posters showing the incredible beauty of the Phoenix Mountains, such as the one seen in the image at right, were used in addition to mailers and flyers to rally support with the simple message "Save The Phoenix Mountains." (Courtesy Gary Driggs.)

SAVE THE PHOENIX MOUNTAINS

Ultimately the proof of these efforts would be found on the ground within the Phoenix Mountains Preserve. Squaw Peak remained the centerpiece of the preserve, and bond funding was essential for improvements to the parking area and to the summit trail itself. This 1989 photograph shows families continuing to enjoy excursions to Squaw Peak for the challenge of the climb and the magnificent views from the summit. (Courtesy Hartz family.)

On March 23, 2003, Arizona native Lori Piestewa was killed in Iraq, becoming the first Native American military woman to be killed in combat. Native Americans had long found the name "Squaw Peak" to be offensive, and in 2003, the mountain was renamed Piestewa Peak. Piestewa Peak remains one of the signature natural wonders within the Phoenix area, with untold thousands visiting the Phoenix Mountains Preserve each year to enjoy the magnificent open space that so many worked so long to preserve. (Courtesy U.S. Army.)

Seven

MCDOWELL SONORAN PRESERVE

The McDowell Sonoran Preserve is a prime example of intensified preservation activity in the 1990s as cities throughout the Phoenix area grew at a tremendous pace in size and population, threatening to engulf the mountains and plow under the Sonoran Desert. However, the McDowell Sonoran Preserve story is more importantly a unique example of grassroots community activists forcing an issue into the public debate, setting audacious preservation goals, generating overwhelming community support, and making it happen. It is also a story of a community so committed to open space preservation that it repeatedly voted to tax itself, with estimates reaching as much as $500 million or more, to compete with deep-pocketed developers in acquiring the land. The story of the creation of the McDowell Sonoran Preserve is not yet over, but its beginning chapters teach powerful lessons.

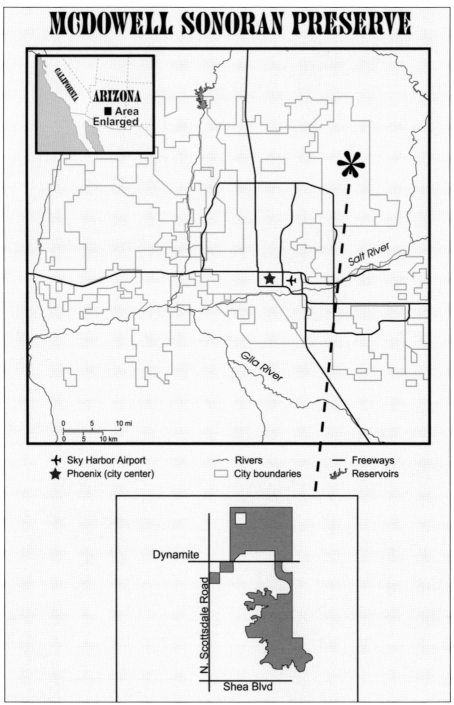

MCDOWELL SONORAN PRESERVE

The McDowell Sonoran Preserve is located in northeastern Scottsdale, north and east of SR101. Currently the Lost Dog Wash access area is the major access point for the preserve, with a full range of amenities for hikers and bikers. It is located north of Via Linda, off of 124th Street. The Sunrise Trailhead has parking at 144th Street and Via Linda. Both access areas are on the southern edge of the preserve. (Map by Donna Hartz.)

The McDowell Mountains dominate the landscape of the northern part of Scottsdale, rising to over 4,000 feet in elevation. The southern portion of the range, including McDowell Mountain (seen in this photograph), are composed of metasedimentary rocks dating from about 1.8 billion years ago. During the late 19th and early 20th centuries, there were several small-scale mining efforts in this part of the McDowells. (Courtesy City of Scottsdale Preservation Division.)

The northern portion of the McDowell Mountains are composed of igneous rocks, more recently uplifted and spectacularly transformed into fantastic shapes by millions of years of erosion. The formation known as Tom's Thumb, easily seen from most of Scottsdale, and pictured above, is a good example of these eroded granitic formations. (Courtesy City of Scottsdale Preservation Division.)

Archeological evidence of human history within the McDowells and on the surrounding deserts indicates a human presence going back some 9,000 years. The McDowells contain numerous spectacular petroglyph sites, as can be seen in the photograph at left. (Courtesy City of Scottsdale Preservation Division.)

The Hohokam were active in the region between about 2,000 and 600 years ago. They quarried basalt from several locations along the southern ridges of the McDowell foothills. Much of the archeological evidence, including the petroglyphs in this photograph, is from the Hohokam era. (Courtesy City of Scottsdale Preservation Division.)

Anglo ranching, mining, and homesteading around the McDowells began perhaps 150 years ago. The first larger-scale activity in the area began during the second decade of the 20th century with one of Scottsdale's first entrepreneurs, E. O. Brown. Brown (seen at right) was a prominent businessman in the little village of Scottsdale and invested in ranch land some 20 miles north of town. (Courtesy Scottsdale Public Library's Southwest Collection.)

Over several decades, E. O. Brown and his son E. E. Brown accumulated tens of thousands of acres in and below the McDowell Mountains. They acquired the DC brand and operated as DC Ranch. As their business grew, so did their ranch headquarters, pictured above at the foot of the northern McDowells. As the mid-20th century approached, E. E. Brown partnered with old friend and fellow entrepreneur Kemper Marley, and the ranch grew to some 43,000 acres—much of what is now the northern part of Scottsdale and the heart of what eventually would become the McDowell Sonoran Preserve. By the last third of the 20th century Scottsdale was growing rapidly in size and population, and the land near and on the McDowell Mountains was ripe for development. (Courtesy Scottsdale Historical Society.)

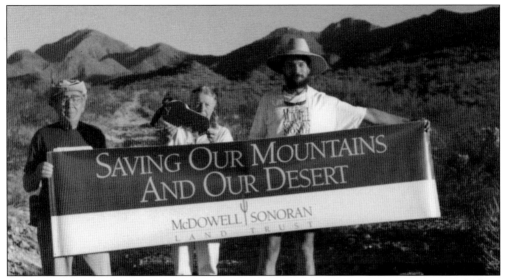

Fortunately not everyone thought that dotting the McDowells with expensive homes and filling the surrounding desert with subdivisions was a great idea. In 1976, the City of Scottsdale attempted to ban development on slopes of 25 degrees or more, but the Arizona Supreme Court struck down that ordinance. It was apparent that zoning was not the best method for preserving the McDowell Mountains, and in the early 1990s, residential development began entering the McDowells. A small group of local residents decided to do something about it before it was too late. Pictured above are three of the early leaders—Chet Andrews, Jane Rau, and Greg Woodall. In 1990, the McDowell Sonoran Land Trust, now the McDowell Sonoran Conservancy, was formed with Carla as executive director and with the goal of "Saving Our Mountains and Our Desert." (Courtesy McDowell Sonoran Conservancy.)

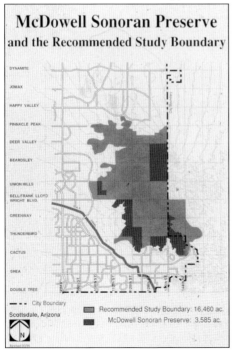

In 1992, the City of Scottsdale appointed a McDowell Mountains Task Force (MMTF) to consider preservation options and approaches. Based upon MMTF recommendations, Scottsdale established the McDowell Sonoran Preserve Commission (MSPC) in 1993 to begin the process of defining the borders of McDowell Sonoran Preserve. Later, in 1993, the commission recommended a preserve targeted at 25.7 square miles. The image at left shows the agreed recommended study boundary for the preserve. (Courtesy City of Scottsdale Preservation Division.)

On October 3, 1994, the Scottsdale City Council held a special meeting at WestWorld, a city-owned facility at the foot of the McDowell Mountains. As seen in this photograph, Mayor Herb Drinkwater led members of the council and other preserve supporters on a tour by horseback to view the spectacular mountain scenery being targeted for preservation. (Courtesy McDowell Sonoran Conservancy.)

The October 3 city council meeting took place with a panoramic view of the McDowell Mountains serving as a dramatic and persuasive backdrop. At the meeting, the council adopted a resolution to formally dedicate the McDowell Sonoran Preserve, initially setting aside four and a half square miles. This included two square miles of city-owned land and two plots of more than one square mile each donated by two developers who were building in the area. Although less than a fifth of the ultimate targeted size, the 2,800-plus acres was an impressive start. (Courtesy McDowell Sonoran Conservancy.)

Unfortunately most of the remaining land targeted for preservation would have to be purchased. In 1994, the MSPC recommended a 0.2 percent sales tax for 30 years to fund land acquisition. The increase in taxes was approved later that year by voters with a 64 percent share of the vote. In 1995, the citizens of Scottsdale again demonstrated their strong support for the McDowell Sonoran Preserve with 73 percent of the voters approving the sale of revenue bonds to accelerate the land purchase process. The photograph from the above campaign mailer reminded the citizens of what they were voting to preserve. (Courtesy McDowell Sonoran Conservancy.)

With money in hand, the City of Scottsdale was able to begin the land acquisition process. The first additional land was acquired in 1997, initiating a long and complex process of negotiations with dozens of individual land owners. But the McDowell Sonoran Preserve was now a reality, growing month by month, and evidenced by signs appearing throughout the desert. (Courtesy City of Scottsdale Preservation Division.)

The 25.7 square miles targeted for preservation in 1993 were dominated by the McDowell Mountains. In 1996, Scottsdale created the Desert Preservation Task Force (DPTF) to consider whether the McDowell Sonoran Preserve should be expanded to preserve more of the Sonoran Desert lands. In 1997, DPTF recommended adding 19,940 acres to the preserve. By 1998, the City of Scottsdale had accepted the DPTF recommendation and had expanded the preserve boundary, as seen at right, to 36,400 acres. This is equal to roughly 57 square miles or about one-third of the total area of Scottsdale. (Courtesy City of Scottsdale Preservation Division.)

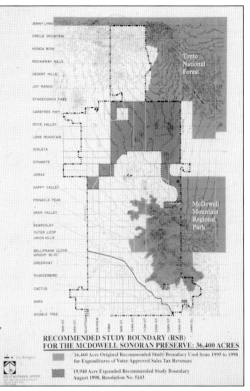

RECOMMENDED STUDY BOUNDARY (RSB)
FOR THE MCDOWELL SONORAN PRESERVE: 36,400 ACRES

16,460 Acre Original Recommended Study Boundary Used from 1995 to 1998 for Expenditures of Voter Approved Sales Tax Revenues

19,940 Acre Expanded Recommended Study Boundary August 1998, Resolution No. 5143

Preserving the desert in addition to the mountains was an important and timely decision. As can be seen from the above photograph, the Sonoran desert in northern Scottsdale contains some truly magnificent scenery, and was more easily developable than much of the remote mountain acreage. Early development activity was already under way. Tens of thousands of acres in northern Scottsdale would be extremely attractive for plowing under the desert for high-priced residential development. (Courtesy City of Scottsdale Preservation Division.)

One of the centerpieces of the proposed preserve was the DC Ranch land, incorporating Windgate Pass and the land below it, owned the Corrigan family, the heirs of Kemper Marley. The contours of the land at Windgate Pass, as seen in the above photograph, made it enticingly developable, including the possibility of residential or commercial development on the pass itself. A master-planned community, DC Ranch, was already being built immediately below this area, and these thousands of acres at the desirable, higher elevations could support many thousands of homes—and would be visible from across the Phoenix area. (Courtesy Hartz family.)

In February 1998, the city concluded four years of negotiations with DC Ranch and reached agreement to acquire 5,275 acres for the preserve. Windgate Pass and 2,685 developable acres were purchased for $95 million, and DC Ranch donated 1,918 acres to the preserve, including three of the highest peaks—Tom's Thumb, McDowell Mountain, and Thompson Peak. This photograph shows the press conference held at DC Ranch to officially announce and celebrate the deal. With this acquisition, some 13,000 acres or 80 percent of the original goal had now been preserved, and the McDowell Sonoran Preserve was now a significant reality. (Courtesy City of Scottsdale Preservation Division.)

Throughout the 1990s, the organization now known as the McDowell Sonoran Conservancy (MSC) worked closely with the City of Scottsdale to ensure the establishment and completion of the preserve, assist in the land acquisition process, promote and celebrate the wonders of the preserve, and support the city in their stewardship of the land. In 1998, the MSC Steward program was created and became an important partner with the city with responsibility for protecting and maintaining the land. A steward's training program was established at Scottsdale Community College, and the first class, pictured above, graduated in the fall of 1998. (Courtesy McDowell Sonoran Conservancy.)

An important part of MSC's Steward training program was education in the field—understanding the flora, fauna, geology, and history of the land that forms the preserve. As the stewards would be regularly interacting with the public and leading hikes into the preserve, ongoing education was of the highest priority. This photograph shows a group of stewards in the preserve as a part of the training program. (Courtesy McDowell Sonoran Conservancy.)

Safe public access to the McDowell Sonoran Preserve was an important priority for the city and the MSC. The stewards play a vital role in that process—patrolling the public access points and trails, and working to keep the trails in a safe condition. This photograph shows Chet Andrews (foreground), then director of the steward program, and other stewards working to keep a trail in good shape. (Courtesy McDowell Sonoran Conservancy.)

Of course, not all trails need be built through the backbreaking labor of stewards or city staff. This photograph shows a Bobcat being used for the early scraping of a new trail. The trail system planned by the City of Scottsdale will provide access to many of the most spectacular areas within the preserve, while maintaining public safety and protecting the safety of the preserve's archeological treasures. (Courtesy City of Scottsdale Preservation Division.)

Another important responsibility of the stewards in cooperation with city staff is keeping the preserve clean. Numerous sections of the preserve had been used to illegally dump garbage, leaving years of accumulated trash throughout the preserve. The stewards constantly organized cleanup projects. In this photograph, from high up the Windgate Pass, preserve manager Claire Miller, center, works with stewards in removing trash. (Courtesy Hartz family.)

Not all trash could be collected in plastic bags or dragged out by the stewards. A number of derelict automobiles were abandoned in the preserve, and the City of Scottsdale arranged for assistance from the Arizona National Guard to remove the wrecks—good training for the National Guard and critical assistance in the cleanup effort. (Courtesy McDowell Sonoran Conservancy.)

The McDowell Sonoran Preserve was never intended as a private playground or privilege for those fortunate to live along its edges. As such, a comprehensive public access plan was an integral part of the preserve plan. However, the wording of the previous tax measures did not allow for its use in the building of public access facilities. In 2004, Scottsdale citizens approved a further .15-percent increase in the sales tax to fund additional land purchases and access area amenities. The first of these access points was opened in late 2004 at the Sunrise Trailhead. The above photograph shows city and MSC leaders at the grand opening ceremony. (Courtesy City of Scottsdale Preservation Division.)

In 2005, the opening of the Lost Dog trailhead was celebrated. In this photograph looking southwest toward Camelback Mountain, the impressive trailhead amenities can be seen. The McDowell Sonoran Preserve remains a work in progress. Essentially all the private land within the boundaries has been acquired, but some 19,000 acres remain State Trust Land. Unfortunately the city may have to compete with developers to acquire the remaining land. Yet the extraordinary preservation achievements since 1990 show what can happen if the people fight for preservation and work in cooperation with their elected public officials. The natural wonders of the Phoenix area can be preserved for generations to come. (Courtesy City of Scottsdale Preservation Division.)

BIBLIOGRAPHY

Blanc, Tara A. *Oasis in the City: The History of the Desert Botanical Garden.* Phoenix: Heritage Publishers, Inc., 2000.

Collins, William S. *The Emerging Metropolis: Phoenix, 1944–1973.* Phoenix: Arizona State Parks Board, 2005.

Driggs, Gary. *Camelback: Sacred Mountain of Phoenix.* Tempe, AZ: Arizona Historical Foundation, 1998.

Gart, James H. *Papago Park: A History of Hole-In-The-Rock from 1848 to 1995.* Phoenix: City of Phoenix Parks, Recreation and Library Department, 1996.

Gober, Patricia. *Metropolitan Phoenix: Place Making and Community Building in the Desert.* Philadelphia: University of Pennsylvania Press, 2006.

Miller, Joseph. "Encanto Park, Phoenix Park Beautiful," *Arizona Highways Magazine,* October 1939.

San Felice, Jack. *Squaw Peak: A Hiker's Guide.* Higley, AZ: Millsite Canyon Publishing, 1997.

Swarth, H. S. *Birds of the Papago Saguaro National Monument.* Washington, D.C.: Government Printing Office, 1920.

Webster, Gertrude D. "Arizona Desert Botanical Garden," *Desert Plant Life,* February 1939.

DISCOVER THOUSANDS OF LOCAL HISTORY BOOKS FEATURING MILLIONS OF VINTAGE IMAGES

Arcadia Publishing, the leading local history publisher in the United States, is committed to making history accessible and meaningful through publishing books that celebrate and preserve the heritage of America's people and places.

Find more books like this at
www.arcadiapublishing.com

Search for your hometown history, your old stomping grounds, and even your favorite sports team.

Consistent with our mission to preserve history on a local level, this book was printed in South Carolina on American-made paper and manufactured entirely in the United States. Products carrying the accredited Forest Stewardship Council (FSC) label are printed on 100 percent FSC-certified paper.

MADE IN THE USA